UNLOCK YOUR RIDING TALENT

with 30 key exercises from Tina Sederholm

David and Charles

A DAVID & CHARLES BOOK
David & Charles is a subsidiary of F+W (UK) Ltd.,
an F+W Publications Inc. company

First published in the UK in 2005

Distributed in North America
by F+W Publications, Inc.
4700 East Galbraith Road
Cincinnati, OH 45236
1-800-289-0963

ISBN 0 7153 1963 9

Printed in China by SNP-Leefung
for David & Charles
Brunel House   Newton Abbot   Devon

ALL PHOTOGRAPHY BY MATTHEW ROBERTS
Line illustrations by Ethan Danielson

Commissioning Editor: Jane Trollope
Desk Editor: Louise Crathorne
Art Editor: Sue Cleave
Project Editor: Jo Weeks
Production Controller: Jennifer Campbell

Visit our website at www.davidandcharles.co.uk

David & Charles books are available from all good bookshops;
alternatively you can contact our Orderline on (0)1626 334555 or write
to us at FREEPOST EX2 110, David & Charles Direct, Newton Abbot,
TQ12 4ZZ (no stamp required UK mainland).

Contents

Introduction

I love learning. I have always been inquisitive about what makes people and horses tick. It is a cliché, but the best days of my life are when I learn something new, or when something I have been working on finally falls into place. Whether this was my nature or my nurture I do not know, but certainly the place I was brought up in and the people I grew up around provided me with an extremely fertile learning ground.

My father, Lars Sederholm, comes from a classical school of training, firstly from his time in the Swedish cavalry and then from his early mentor Henri St. Cyr, winner of four Olympic gold medals for dressage. Until I was in my thirties, my parents owned and ran the world famous Waterstock House Training Centre, a place where my father's classical training met the world of competition, and that attracted both distinguished and aspiring riders. For over 40 years, my father trained some of the best riders in a variety of disciplines – show jumpers such as Michael Whitaker, Caroline Bradley and Derek Ricketts, and event riders like William Fox-Pitt, David O'Connor and Yogi Breisner all came for training at different times in their careers. In addition, Waterstock was populated with young riders doing their apprenticeship in the horse world, eager to follow in the footsteps of their heroes. We also had a huge variety of horses in for training, not just from the world of show jumping and horse trials, but also racehorses, dressage horses, hunters, riding club horses, in fact just about every sort of horse you could imagine.

So the atmosphere I grew up in was highly disciplined and motivated; it promoted good horsemanship and a clear understanding of how the horse and rider could work together to achieve the best results. However this was not my only education: over the years, my father sent me to several well respected riders and trainers to soak up different methodologies and ideas.

I started teaching full time in my late teens. I had no formal qualifications, but I had already received, and continued to receive, many hours of tuition from a variety of knowledgeable trainers. I also watched others both teaching and being taught. Although I was not fully conscious of it at the time I was being immersed in the skill of teaching, as well as the actual training of horses and riders, and gaining invaluable experience from my competitive exploits.

About this book

The education at Waterstock was divided into three categories: work on the rider, work on the horse and work on the combination. Great emphasis was put on improving the rider's seat and application of their aids, together with giving them an appreciation of how their body and that of their horse worked. It was only when the rider was capable of giving the horse 'a good ride' that they were introduced to the ways of educating a horse. That education was based on the belief that every individual animal has a natural way of going, and that his training should be an extension of that. This meant that even when the horse progressed to a high level of training, it was never at the expense of what my father says is 'the way the Creator intended him to use himself'.

This book follows the same basic theories. The first section details many exercises that will improve the rider's seat, by developing their balance, sense of rhythm, flexibility and feel. A high percentage of problems that riders come up against can be resolved by improving their seat and developing their awareness of what is happening underneath them. These problems are not so much the fault of the horse, who often gets the blame, but occur because of a rider's ignorance or misunderstanding of the way the horse functions.

The seat exercises range from the simple to more advanced levels of difficulty. This is because learning to ride well is an on-going process. When riders know more about how to educate horses, there is a tendency for them to forget that they are also athletes who need continuous training. The truth is that even experienced riders need to monitor their seat and application of their aids, and be reminded, periodically, of the basics.

After the section on the seat, I concentrate on exercises that will help the rider learn how to educate the horse and themselves on the flat and over fences. Developed with an appreciation of the horse's physiology and psychology, these will hone good riding

skills until they become second nature. They will also prepare the horse and rider for riding good dressage tests and making confident jumping rounds.

These exercises also start in a simple form and then build up. In my experience, the horse and rider learn most effectively when information is given in small, easily digestible steps. You will find that whenever you or the horse learn something new, even if it is a small thing, you are filled with a feeling of satisfaction and your confidence increases. These easy victories grow into a solid foundation of understanding and confidence. This gives the rider the resources to deal with the inevitable ups and downs that come their way. Although most of the basic exercises are suitable for all riders, a few are aimed at those working towards higher levels of competition.

Time and time again I have seen these exercises bring about positive results, because they give the rider specific, well-defined ways to develop the skills they need. They all originate from the work at Waterstock, and are the result of many hours of listening, watching and practising, on the part of the thousands of pupils and horses who trained with my father, the trainers he educated, and by myself. Pay attention to doing them well, and you will find that they will continue to influence your riding in positive ways, long after you first tried them out.

cherish the little victories

Nearly all of us have the desire to win big competitions and cover ourselves with glory at some point in our lives. It is good to have goals like that for they help us strive to become better. Eventually though, you will find it is what you learn along the way, the little victories that you achieve every day, that bring you the most consistent pleasure. I hope this book will provide you with many such victories and that these will lead you to bigger victories in the ring, and beyond.

IMPROVING YOUR SEAT

A well-balanced and effective seat is the foundation for any successful rider. There is nothing more pleasing to see than a rider who looks completely at one with their horse, communicating in a subtle but clear way so the horse responds willingly and with elegance. Not all riders are aware of how much their seat and aids impact on the horse, but in my experience, a shortcoming in the seat or balance is often at the root of a breakdown in communication between the rider and the horse.

With this collection of exercises, my aim is to show you how your seat can work with the horse's natural way of going, so that it either allows the horse to operate 'in the way the Creator intended', or works with that movement to make more of it. The exercises are directed at the rider who wants to do both flatwork and jumping, and so they are designed to promote an all-round seat, one from which you could do dressage, or show jumping, or cross country. I am sure you will have noticed that the seat of a pure dressage rider looks very different

GIVE CLEARER MESSAGES, GET BETTER RESPONSES

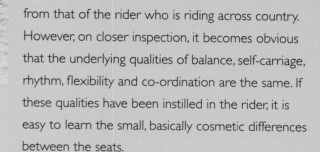

from that of the rider who is riding across country. However, on closer inspection, it becomes obvious that the underlying qualities of balance, self-carriage, rhythm, flexibility and co-ordination are the same. If these qualities have been instilled in the rider, it is easy to learn the small, basically cosmetic differences between the seats.

When to do seat work

Whether you are a novice or an experienced rider, it is a good idea to incorporate some work on your seat into your daily training. It can be as simple as taking your legs away a few times to ensure you are sitting in the middle of the horse, to basing most of your session on riding with short stirrups. Personally, I like to start nearly every lesson I give with a quick seat exercise, especially if I spot any tension in the rider when they come into the school. Doing this also helps to encourage them to focus on the lesson and usually guarantees us a good start to our work.

As these exercises concentrate primarily on the rider, it is beneficial for them to be done in an enclosed area or on the lunge. This will give you the chance to concentrate more on yourself while you are working on your seat. It is vital that the horse is connected up as it is almost impossible to sit well on a hollow-backed horse whose head is in the air. If your horse does not easily stay in shape, it is a good idea to use an artificial aid that does not involve the rider's hands, like a bungee rein or a standing martingale. This lets you focus completely on what you are doing, rather than also having to think about keeping the horse together. This is especially important for you if the effort of putting the horse on the bit is something that brings tension into your riding.

Why do seat work?

Although these exercises are focused primarily on the rider, they will also indirectly have a positive effect on many horses, simply because of the improvement that occurs in the rider. In addition, as you become more experienced, it is possible to work on the horse and rider at the same time, as you will see from the more advanced versions of the exercises.

It is worth remembering that many of these exercises are a means to an end, rather than an end in themselves. From time to time you will be asked to do something you would never do in a competition, but be reassured that it will teach you a feel or technique that can be absorbed into your normal riding. For example, you would never go into the ring, standing up straight in your stirrups. However, what you *would* take with you is

➤CHECKPOINT
People get tense in different ways: some tighten their shoulders, others become rigid with their hands, or their breathing can be come shallow and hurried. When someone is trying to do something that they find or think is difficult, they will often get wound up and tense in their bodies. In other words, they try too hard, and this tension works against them achieving the desired result – if a horse feels tension from the rider trying to get him on the bit, he is less likely to do as requested.

Rules of the road

- Let yourself learn in increments. Master something in walk before you try it in trot. If you have a problem in trot, go back to walk, until you have found yourself again.

- Either ride an established horse who is easy to keep together, or use some artificial help such as bungee reins (below).

- Ensure the horse genuinely draws forward.

- Keep breathing. Many people hold their breath when they are trying to control their bodies. However this just encourages tension.

- Be in an enclosed area, or on the lunge.

the sensation of body control that you learnt through doing that exercise.

Time spent working on improving your seat is a sound investment in your future riding success. There is still more to learn on how to influence and educate the horse in a positive way on the flat and jumping, which I will look at later on. Right now though, we will concentrate on the rider, for although some of us are born with more natural balance and feel than others, none of us are so good that we would not benefit from some improvement.

Short stirrup work

Looking after your balance when you are riding is a bit like looking after your bank account. The more money you pay in to your bank account, the more money you have; the more consistent your balance is, the more trust the horse will have in you, and the more mentally relaxed he will become. However, losses of balance by the rider debit that account of confidence.

Every time you lose your balance, even in a minor way, you affect the horse's balance, too. If this situation happens a lot, the horse will become unsettled, and will defend himself against the rider's movements and become tight and resistant, rather than co-operating with their requests.

Working with short stirrups is invaluable because it will quickly make you fitter and stronger. It will also considerably improve your balance and flexibility, which will make you feel a more competent rider, especially when you go back to the luxury of normal length stirrups.

The basic exercise – two-point seat

There are many degrees of having your seat out of the saddle: you can have your bottom right up in the air, like a jockey, or it can be virtually grazing the saddle, like some show-jumping riders. The position I am going to explain here is similar to a jumping position, but to avoid confusion, I have called it the 'two-point seat', so that you recognize it as a training position.

■ Shorten up your stirrups by four or five holes and you immediately become more aware of when you are in balance and when you are not and, because you feel a little vulnerable, you will automatically take more care of what you are doing with your bodyweight. Short stirrups also increase a rider's flexibility. You need to have supple hip, knee and ankle joints in order to absorb the movement of the horse – vital if you are to keep your balance.

practice in halt

When you first try this position, practice it in halt (right) so that you get the mechanics correct. Once you have found your balance in the halt, you can practice coming back down into the middle of the saddle in a soft and controlled way. Do this by bending your joints and allowing your knee to come slightly away from the saddle, with the kneecap travelling diagonally down towards the ground. At the same time, let your shoulders come back to a vertical position, and allow your bottom come into the deepest part of the saddle.

■ Think of your joints being like the suspension of a car absorbing the undulations of the road to give the passengers a smooth ride. Stiff joints cause a rider to lose their balance easily because rather than absorbing the horse's movement they bounce off it.

A good lower leg position is the key to keeping your balance when you have your seat out of the saddle. The most effective place for the lower leg to be is at the girth. The stirrup leathers hang perpendicular and the rider has the stirrup on the ball of their foot. Aim to have approximately the same amount of bend in your three leg joints – hip, knee, ankle – with the weight going down through your head. Your upper body is inclined forward in a controlled way from the hip, and your bottom is about 20cm (8in) clear of the saddle. Your hands rest on the horse's neck so that they are stable, but they only take minimal amount of your weight; in no way should you be leaning against the horse's neck.

■ Once you have got a feel for it in halt, try the two-point position in walk and trot (above). Spring up into the two-point position and stay there for about five strides, making sure you establish your balance. Then come back into the saddle lightly. If the horse flinches or speeds up as you do this, it is an indication that you have come down too heavily or lost your balance, so come down with more care next time. Only practice this exercise in walk long enough for you to feel comfortable; it is most valuable in trot and canter, when you have more forward movement underneath you to absorb.

13

Change of scene

■ Intersperse work on the two-point seat with some rising trot and some canter work with you sitting on the horse.

You will find that the short stirrups encourage you to sit more vertically and carry yourself more elegantly. This exercise will also help you improve your lateral balance – that is noticing and correcting yourself if you lean more to one side than the other.

Testing your balance

Once you are comfortable with moving in and out of the two-point seat, you can test your balance in other ways. Establish your balance in the two-point seat and then take one hand off the horse's neck and place it just below your waist (right). After about six strides, change hands. Repeat this exercise several times, before coming back to rising trot. This will also test your co-ordination, revealing whether you can maintain your balance while carrying out a simple task. The horse's rhythm should stay the same while you change hands. If the horse speeds up as you go from one hand to the other, it is an indication that you lost your balance.

drawing forward

The horse must draw forward genuinely for this work to be effective. I liken this feeling to a boat with wind in its sails. If the horse is not drawing forward in a true way, the rider will find themselves ahead of the movement and it will be almost impossible to keep their balance. If you find the horse is behind your aids, give him a friendly nudge with your heels so you get him back in front of your leg. If the horse is consistently unwilling to go forward, you must attend to that before doing any other work with him.

Advanced exercise

Half-halts in the two-point seat

When you are able to consistently keep your balance in the two-point position, you can start to work on the horse at the same time as testing your balance. This work is done in trot and canter, and generally the shorter the rider's stirrups are, the better. You will also find, the shorter your stirrups are, the further your seat needs to be out of the saddle.

■ Go into the two-point position and bridge your reins (opposite).
■ At specified places in the school, say A, B, C and E, ask the horse for a simple collection for a few strides by closing your hands around the reins. Make sure you maintain your balance while closing your hands, and then encourage the horse forward in an improved rhythm.
■ The horse may stiffen his jaw when he is first asked for the collection. However, if you remain consistent in your balance and use a sensitive hand, he will give in his jaw after a few attempts.

■ When his jaw gives and he responds to your closing hand, the horse will also collect himself in an uncomplicated way, and his rhythm will be accentuated. At this point, soften your hands and, because your stirrups are very short, use your voice (click with your tongue) to emphasize the good rhythm. This is as necessary as putting your foot on the accelerator after changing gear in the car.
■ The bonus here is that because you are standing in the stirrups, the horse has plenty of room for his back to round and to put his hindlegs underneath. His back becomes soft and flexible, so that when you thereafter sit on him, you will find that he feels loose and springy and is a pleasure to sit on.

> ➤CHECKPOINT
> *Riding with short stirrups is quite tough on the rider physically. Therefore, when you first try it, do only about 10–15 minutes before moving onto another exercise, either to improve your seat, for example, taking your legs away (p.24), or practise one that focuses more on the horse.*

bridging the reins

When you bridge the reins, you put one rein on top of the other (1) in between both your hands (2) so that they form a small hoop (3) that fits over the horse's neck (4).

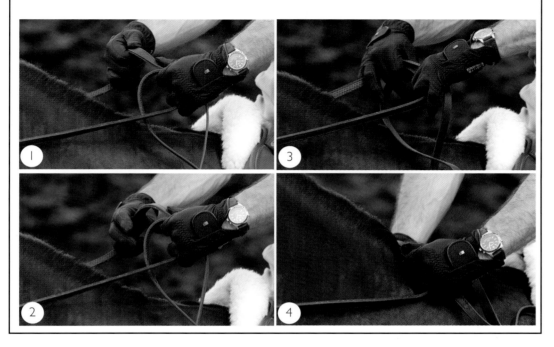

Standing up straight

Have you ever noticed that well-balanced riders have an inner strength and stillness running through them? Think of Rodrigo Pessoa or Billy Twomey in show jumping; they have the ability to land after a huge fence and be in perfect balance.

Or perhaps Andrew Nicholson and William Fox-Pitt; their horses seem to gallop effortlessly underneath them, and should they hit a cross-country fence, they recover within a stride from a mistake which would have had most riders on the floor. All these riders combine a core stability with immense flexibility. Of course, not all riders are going to reach these heights, but if you can attain even a touch of this stability, you will both feel more secure as a rider, and your horse will feel more confident in you. This exercise will introduce you to that feeling, as well as testing your balance in an alternative way to the two-point position work. It is best done with jumping-length stirrups, though if you get proficient at it, you can always try it with short ones too.

> **►CHECKPOINT**
> *If you have a friend on the ground, ask them to stand in front of you, so they can check that you are level. They will be able to tell you if both your feet are pointing forwards and if you have equal weight in your stirrups. It is not uncommon for a rider to turn one leg in a different direction from the other (right). Simply getting the weight even on the balls of your feet and having both of them facing forwards can have a ripple effect through the rest of the body, so that everything levels out.*

The basic exercise

■ In halt, spring upwards into a standing position, with your legs straight and your top body as vertical as you can get it without falling backwards. Hold a piece of mane, as it is quite a test to keep your balance in this position for more than a few seconds. Check that you are as tall as possible. Riders often think they are standing straight, when, in fact, they are pinching the saddle with their knees or tipping forward at the hips.

■ While you are in this position, you also have an excellent opportunity to get more depth into your heels, so once you have found your balance, let go in your ankles and allow your weight to drop down into your heels a little further.

■ Once you have found your balance, and dropped more weight into your heels, you can lower yourself back into the middle of the saddle with control and care.

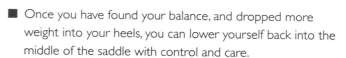

■ Allow your lower legs to fold around the horse and bend your knees so that your seat comes down in the middle of the saddle.

On the move

The next stage is to stand up straight with some movement underneath you. In walk, spring up and find your balance in the standing position. Although your hips and knees are straight, keep the elasticity in your ankles so you can absorb the horse's movement. Remain here for a few strides before coming back down into the saddle. Remember to keep breathing normally. Often when riders are trying to keep their balance, they forget to breathe, this makes them rigid and this rigidity causes them to fall back into the saddle.

It is also vital that you make sure the horse is genuinely drawing forward (p.14), because it is nearly impossible to keep your balance on a horse that is going in a grudging way. The mechanics of the exercise mean that you are not able to push strongly, so use your voice if necessary to keep the horse travelling in a straight line.

Once you are familiar with standing up straight at walk, it is often easier to do it in trot because the horse draws forward more naturally. However, even when you are in trot, do not try to influence the horse to be in shape. There is great benefit to be had from letting him trot around on a semi-loose rein with you standing up straight in perfect balance. You will find that a sharp horse will often slow down and move in a level balance underneath you, and it is good to recognize how the horse can become square over his feet, simply because you are well-balanced on top of him.

Advanced exercises

Finding your balance in walk and trot in this position and being able to hold it for several strides before returning to the saddle in a controlled way is quite an achievement in itself. However, here are some more ways you can use standing up straight, if it is an exercise that suits you.

■ Try it in canter. When this is done well, you can get a lovely feeling of the horse carrying himself in a natural balance underneath you, with no pressure.

■ Trot over a single or set of three poles in the standing up straight position (above). This will help train your body control into a fence and it will also increase your ability to absorb the horse's movement.

■ Once you are confident in this position, and if you are sitting on an experienced horse, you can even jump a few small fences from trot and canter, to get the feeling of maintaining your balance into the fence. Go with the horse in a normal way over the

exercise notes

It is important to remember that this position is an exercise you learn as a means to an end, rather than an end in itself. It will make you familiar with the core stability and body control that you will use when you want to collect the horse on the flat or ask him to 'wait' in front of a fence. It gives you the feeling of being the mast of a ship, and that however the ship might rock around, you will remain in the middle of it, as a balancing factor. Quite simply, when you are well-balanced and have this body control, the horse will find it easier to keep his balance, and therefore be in a much better position to carry out your requests.

square over the feet

Square over the feet is another way to describe the feeling of the horse being in balance and having an even footfall (often you can hear this — there is the same stress on each hoofbeat). Just as a human being can stand square, with even weight over his feet, giving the sense of being solid and grounded, so can a horse. When the horse (or human) moves, this feeling translates into regular and definite footsteps. The opposite is when the horse is running away, or hanging behind the rider.

fence and then see if you can stand up straight directly after the fence.

■ Co-ordinate standing up straight with 'Legs away' (p.24). Once you have stood up straight and found your balance, come back into the middle of the saddle. As soon as you touch the saddle, lift your legs away from the hip joint and hold them away for a few seconds, then let them come softly back around the horse.

Standing and sitting in canter

This exercise is one of the most useful I ever learnt in my career as a jumping rider. It tests the rider's co-ordination and develops their adaptability, especially important in the jumping rider who needs to be comfortable with having their seat both in and out of the saddle. Most significantly, it establishes a sense of rhythm in the horse and rider.

Watching good show jumpers, I am often struck by the tremendous lift and rhythm there is in their horse's canter, and the lightness and flexibility of their seat. When it is done well, this exercise will help you to encourage that suspension in the horse's stride and the athleticism in your seat and this will prepare you physically to respond swiftly to what is happening underneath you while jumping. It will also help you to identify your horse's natural rhythm, and then you can accentuate and build on it to produce a canter that is elastic and powerful.

Once learnt, this exercise is an easy way to put spring back into the rider and rhythm back into the horse, and I regularly ask a rider to 'stand and sit' after jumping a fence in order to train these qualities into them.

in front of the aids

This refers to the horse responding forward in a genuine way, both physically and mentally. Often, a horse can seem to be moving forward, but is in fact mentally switched off, so when the rider asks him to do something new or unfamiliar, he responds in an unwilling fashion. Therefore, it is necessary to start all training sessions by testing the horse's response to your leg, so that you know he is mentally and physically with you before starting your schooling work.

The basic exercise

You need to be familiar with the two-point position (p.12) before you try this exercise. You will not be coming as far out of the saddle as you might do in the two-point exercise, but your joints do need to be flexible, and you need to be confident about finding your balance with your seat out of the saddle.

■ The idea of this exercise is that you stand and sit for a set number of strides, in canter, on a circle, several times in succession. A good way to start is to sit for four strides and stand for four strides.

- It is important that you are conscientious about sticking to the same number of strides in order to tune into the rhythm. If you sit for five, stand for three, then sit for four, the effect will be disjointed.
- Experiment with the number of strides that you stand and sit for. Try three and three, and two and two. If you need to get more lightness into your seat, you can stand for four and sit for two.
- Later on, standing and sitting is incorporated into some of the jumping exercises (p.98), so it is a good idea to learn the technique now, so it is a natural part of your abilities when you come to do it in connection with jumping.

> ➤ **CHECKPOINT**
> *Pay attention to the lightness of your seat. Your bottom should only come a few centimetres out of the saddle, and then graze lightly on the saddle for the sitting strides. Make sure your horse is always in front of your aids. This means that when you are sitting you may need to use your voice or nudge him with your heels to make sure he remains in front of your aids when you come out of the saddle.*

Legs away – going with the flow

If you pick only one exercise to learn in this whole book, I recommend that it is this one, because it has such a profound effect on the rider and their application of the aids.

Have you ever watched a skilled rider and marvelled at how at one they seem with the horse? Sometimes they can give the illusion that they are not moving at all. Yet the reality is that they *are* moving. They are consistently following and absorbing the horse's movement, and it is this which creates the impression that they are sitting still. There are many small muscle movements that go on all the time that enable the rider to absorb the horse's action. It is not necessary to know all the ins and outs of these movements. What is more important is that you create the willingness in your seat to follow whatever happens underneath you. Once you can do that, you can then use your seat to greater effect to influence the horse.

'Legs away' was one of the exercises we used most widely at Waterstock, and one of its many benefits is that while doing it, the rider experiences the feeling of their seat following the horse's movement in a completely natural way, without any force.

This exercise takes a little bit of thought and practice to do well, but the benefits far outweigh the effort you put in to it. It can also be used, as you will see in later exercises, to help you learn the correct timing of aids for a half-halt, and prepare to go through a corner in a relaxed way, as well as being a quick way to re-align your seat whenever necessary.

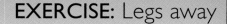

The basic exercise

- Sitting comfortably on the horse, raise your knees slightly and lift both legs from the hips, away from the saddle (far left).
- Hold your legs there for three or four seconds, and then let them return to the horse's sides in a controlled way.
- At first, you may only be able to take your legs a few centimetres away, but after several repetitions, your hips will let go, and you will feel looser and freer. You may also find it useful to put a couple of fingers under the pommel to give yourself some stability, especially when you first attempt this exercise in trot. The technique is exactly the same in trot and canter as it is in walk, but the increased movement makes it more testing — just as sitting trot is more difficult than sitting on a horse in walk.

> ►CHECKPOINT
> *It is important that you keep yourself vertical throughout this exercise, rather than throwing your upper body back and using the momentum to kick the legs out. If you do this, the horse will let you know by hollowing his back and quickening his pace because you have become a cause of discomfort.*

the domino effect

The hips are the major joints involved with absorbing the motion of the horse. They are ball and socket joints, which means they have the potential for a great range of movement. However, many people do not make much use of these joints in their everyday lives, so they tighten up, then when they sit on a horse, the hips do not open and close with the horse's movement. This causes tension in the pelvic girdle and makes them bounce in the saddle.

'Legs away' encourages the hips to let go. Once this happens, the rider's seat settles on the horse's back, travelling fluidly with his movement. This has a domino effect through the rest of the rider's body — the front of the body opens up, the back becomes engaged, the legs relax and can lie in a friendly way on the horse's sides, see p.26.

Taking it further

Once you have got the feel for legs away, you can test yourself in two different ways.

- You can either keep your legs away for a few strides longer than you have previously done, or you can do several quick legs away in a row, in a similar way to Mark Todd (see 'celebrity use'). The relaxation in your legs that follows will make it easier to sit to the trot, and for you to push the horse forward in a relaxed way.
- You can also experiment with doing legs away both with and without stirrups. Taking your legs away without stirrups encourages you to have even more length in your legs, so that you can get the feeling of hugging the horse with a friendly leg.

friendly legs

One of the ways a rider communicates with a horse is by using varying amounts of leg pressure. A 'friendly' leg describes the feel with which the rider encourages the horse to go forward, and indicates that the sensitivity needed when using the leg is comparable to the sensitivity required from the rider's hands.

Advanced exercises

Circling the arm and looking away

Another result of our sedentary lifestyle is that our bodies get curled forward and compressed. As you are freeing up the bottom half of your body, it makes sense to loosen and open the top half as well. Once you have practised legs away a few times, you can add the following elements to the exercise.

1 Put the reins in one hand and circle the other arm backwards. Make sure your arm is straight at the elbow and the fingers are stretched in a relaxed way.
2 When you reach the top of the circle (when your arm is behind your ear) hold your arm still and take your legs away for a couple of strides.
3 Once you have replaced your legs, you can finish the circle.

26

4 Change hands and do the same with the opposite arm circling. Take your time doing this exercise so that you get the full benefit of your arm lengthening your upper body and the legs away undoing your hip joints.

The third element of this exercise is to look in the opposite direction at the same time as you do the other two actions. It works best if you do it in the order below.

1 Circle your left arm, stop at the top and turn your head to the right (left).

2 Take your legs away for three strides.

3 Allow your legs to come softly back around the horse's sides.

4 Turn your head to look straight forward.

5 Finish the circle. Repeat with the other arm. As well as stretching your body and adding elegance to your riding, you will find this exercise also does wonders for your co-ordination.

celebrity use

At competitions, I often saw Mark Todd using the legs away exercise when he was warming up for a dressage test. He would make a halt, take his legs away from the saddle three or four times in quick succession and then ride off again. I am sure he did this because he felt the benefits of freeing up his legs and putting them back around the horse in a fresh and friendly way: often it is not until you free your legs up, that you realize how much tension has crept into them.

Levelling out the rider

There is always a lot of talk about whether the horse is even on both reins and level in the rider's hands. But what if the rider is unlevel? All of us favour one side over the other, and horses will adapt themselves to our inconsistencies, as well as having inconsistencies of their own.

Unlevelness often occurs in a rider's seat when their focus is on schooling the horse. In their efforts to achieve what they want, unhelpful habits creep in and detract from what they are trying to do. Checking in periodically with yourself about the levelness of your seat, and asking yourself if you may be the cause of any resistance in your horse can save you a lot of unnecessary battling.

Unlevelness in the rider comes out in different ways. Some people are stiffer in one side of their body than the other, others collapse to one side. Some combine the two. Correct the unlevelness in one area though, and it will often have a domino effect throughout the rider's body, smoothing out other inconsistencies in their lateral balance.

I have found that straightness in the horse and levelness in the rider's lateral balance are two things that need to be worked on constantly, so here are a couple of exercises you can use to help you to even out your body.

One stirrup shorter than the other

Many riders put more weight on one seatbone than the other, and then lean in the other way to compensate, collapsing at the waist. Sometimes one part of our body can simply feel heavier than the other, even when we are standing on the ground. This exercise will help rectify these imbalances.

■ Firstly you need to identify which side you are collapsing on. This is usually quite easy for someone on the ground to see, and is most obvious on the circle, when the rider's weight sits on the outside of the saddle, or they look as if they have been punched in the side, with their head tipping in (right). Another sign to look out for is that the horse will tend to speed up and cut in to compensate for the rider's collapsed side. So if he tends to stiffen and cut in on the right circle, he is letting you know that you are collapsing that way.

■ If you are collapsing to the right, the solution is to make your left stirrup four or five holes shorter than your right (below) and ride like this for a while. There should be a significant difference between the two stirrup lengths in order to make an impression on the rider. Shortening the stirrup on the

side where the rider shifts to the outside effectively 'shortens' that side of the rider, causing the collapsing side to 'lengthen'. When you ride like this on both reins, though principally with the shorter stirrup on the outside, you will find that, once you stop fighting the shorter stirrup, you shift internally. It is as if the side that has been falling out is too full, and some of that weight has to be filtered to the emptier side.

- The acid test comes in canter on the circle (below). With this exercise you get a strong sensation of what lengthening the inside leg – which so many instructors spend a lot of time talking about – really feels like.

- When you feel a significant change in your body, you can go back to riding with level stirrups. You will need to pay attention that you do not start to slip back into your old habit. However, as you now have the reference point of a new feel, it will be easier to self-correct.

lateral balance

It is a common mistake to think of balance only in terms of whether the rider is behind or in front of the horse's movement. You must also be aware of your balance laterally – left and right. Riders can be unbalanced by sitting lopsided, or leaning to one side or the other, or putting more weight in one stirrup than the other. Paying attention to your lateral balance, both by doing the following exercises, and by regularly checking your stirrups and making sure you keep sitting evenly on your seatbones, will ensure that it is just as good as your linear balance.

- If you are still finding it hard to sit level on certain parts of the circle, look to the outside just before you get to that area and keep your head turned that way for several strides (above). Looking to the outside alters the position of your body so that your inside hip slides slightly forward. You will now move in sync with the horse's inside hip, which is also slightly further forward in the canter. Your body is now moving in harmony with your horse's body, and this can have a profound effect over any stiffness in him. He will have nothing to resist and therefore will often let go and become softer in his stride and his side, simply because his rider is now correctly positioned.

Carrying the stick

A key area where riders often have problems being level is in their hands. One hand may be in the correct place while the other is heading south towards the rider's knee, or one hand might be much stronger than the other. Unlevel hands make the horse one-sided, and denote a lack of co-ordination in the rider that makes it difficult for them to communicate clearly with the horse. Carrying a stick in front of you will help lessen these issues.

you will need

For this exercise you will need a stick, preferably wooden, about 50cm (20in) long and thin enough for you to get your hands comfortably around it. Part of an old broom handle is ideal. Hold the stick horizontally with your hands about 20cm (8in) apart and your reins as normal.

making a lasting impression

My father has this theory about straightening up. Imagine you have an iron bar that is turned up at the ends. In order to get it straight, it is not enough to press the ends to the horizontal, for when you let go they would still pop up slightly. You need to bend the ends downwards, past the point they need to be, so that when you let go, the bar will become straight. It is the same with the human body. Sometimes we need to push it quite strongly in the opposite direction to which it is accustomed to being, in order to make a lasting impression.

■ Start by riding in walk and trot, making simple turns, circles and straight lines (below). You will find that the stick has a variety of effects. Firstly you will find it easier to keep your hands more level, because it is so obvious when they are not. Through the turns, you will automatically give enough on the outside for the horse to stretch the outside of his body, while still maintaining a forward-thinking contact. In addition, after riding with consistently level hands for a few minutes, other imbalances in your body will even out.

■ Another interesting way to experiment with the stick

is to use it while doing lateral movements. Make a shoulder-in in walk for about 10m (30ft) down the long side, and in a similar way to the turns, you will find yourself automatically positioning your hands correctly. The stick will also counteract any tendency you might have to pull back in a sideways movement, thus allowing the horse to keep moving forwards more easily through it.

■ Make sure you shorten your reins at regular intervals: it is an integral part of riding that the rider needs to adjust the length of their reins many times while they are riding, yet many riders become lazy about this and end up with their hands in their stomach. However, with a stick in front of you, it becomes quite obvious when your reins have got too long, and your hands are unable to compensate by dropping down.

Hold your reins like frying pans

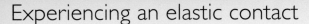

The previous exercise, riding with a horizontal stick in your hands, not only levels you out, but also assists you in creating an even contact. This exercise, holding the reins as if you are holding two frying pans, will take the idea of the elastic contact further.

forward-thinking contact

What are the qualities of a forward-thinking contact? It is elastic, consistent and although you have a feel on the horse's mouth through the rein, you are letting him take the contact from you, rather than creating it by your hand thinking backwards. Think of it like a good handshake – when someone encloses your hand in a light yet comfortable and friendly way you instantly feel at ease with them.

The traditional way to hold the reins is between your ring finger and little finger. In this area you have the capacity to be sensitive by using small movements in your ring finger and to be strong by using the leverage of your whole hand. This leverage can be used in a positive and a negative way. Unfortunately, many riders resort to the negative way in their efforts to either control their horse, or put him on the bit. They do this by tilting the hand back with their little finger back towards their body and this creates a dragging effect on the horse's mouth. The rider ends up holding the horse in place, creating rigidity throughout the horse's frame, and inhibiting his natural movement.

Of course, the way you hold the reins is only one side of the coin. The other side is that you move the horse forwards into that sensitive and responsive hand. However, these exercises can break the cycle of the backward-thinking hand, which, once the rider has got into, can be difficult to change without radical assistance.

arms around your body

A common fault is for riders to be rigid and restricted in their arm movements. You can make your arm movements much more athletic and easier for the horse to accept if you allow your arms the freedom to go around your body, that is that your elbows are free to go past your hip if necessary.

The basic exercise

■ In my teaching I often resort to some unusual tactics to help riders get a particular feel. To introduce the rider to a better quality of forward-thinking elastic contact, I ask them to ride with the reins between their thumbs and first fingers, similar to the way you would hold a frying pan (inset left). Allow yourself a few moments to become familiar with the reins in this position, then school the horse as you normally do, maintaining this hold. You will find that it is easier to have forward-thinking hands because you are no longer tilting them backwards. You will also find that your contact has a more even quality, and in turn, the horse is likely to become more level in his mouth.

■ In addition, you can use this technique to practise making certain moves in a new way. For example, when you make half-halts and transitions, you can experiment by moving your arms around your body in a springy way, so instead of closing your hand, you influence the horse with a take and give action. If you want to put that into a real life context, watch a good show jumper in the ring. In the approach to the fence they may make several checks, taking and giving, within the space of a stride, which creates an elastic ripple through the horse's body. This technique keeps the necessary spring in his stride so the horse can make a good effort over the fence. The action of the rider's arm is reflected in the horse's body.

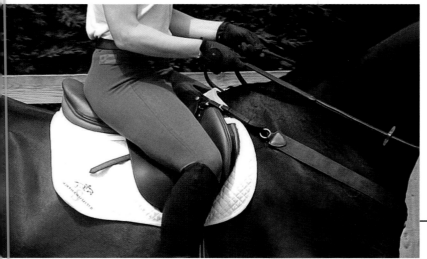

■ Using your arms around your body also automatically encourages you to engage your back in the correct way in a downward transition. As your arms move around your body, your chest and hip area will open, allowing you to come deeper around the horse as he changes pace.

33

Advanced exercises

Crossed reins

You can take this concept further by riding with crossed reins. All human beings favour one side over the other, and these imbalances become reflected in our horses. Riding with crossed reins helps you even out those imbalances, and obliges you to ride the horse more with your seat and legs, rather than just hand contact.

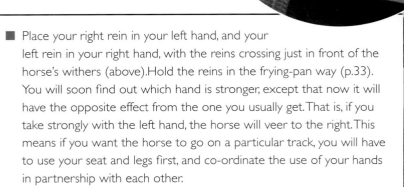

- Place your right rein in your left hand, and your left rein in your right hand, with the reins crossing just in front of the horse's withers (above). Hold the reins in the frying-pan way (p.33). You will soon find out which hand is stronger, except that now it will have the opposite effect from the one you usually get. That is, if you take strongly with the left hand, the horse will veer to the right. This means if you want the horse to go on a particular track, you will have to use your seat and legs first, and co-ordinate the use of your hands in partnership with each other.

the importance of seat and legs

One of the major mental turnarounds that all riders need to make is to learn to use their seat and legs first, before they use their hands. As human beings we are used to doing the majority of tasks with our hands; unless we are used to playing a sport like football, we only use our legs for uncomplicated things like walking and running. However, when you are riding, your hands only influence the horse's head and neck. Your seat and legs direct the other two thirds of him. Therefore, we need to retrain ourselves to move from the default action of fixing everything with our hands, and to become aware of starting most communications with the horse with the legs or seat. When you gain this awareness, you can start to co-ordinate your seat, hands and legs to communicate with the horse, rather than allowing your hands to dominate affairs.

Three to the left, three to the right, three chicken wings

You often hear that a good rider has 'independent' hands. This means that they are able to move and use their arms and hands without it affecting their balance. This is vital if you are going to give the horse clear messages.

Even experienced riders can feel inhibited about moving their arms freely and easily, and so it is a good idea to practise moving them in an independent forward-thinking way without necessarily trying to influence the horse. This exercise teaches you to move your arm independently of your body, and also helps you become familiar and confident with the leading rein, as used in a turn, and the opening rein, which you might use on the outside of a bend. It also highlights the rider's sense of rhythm because of the timing of the movement of the hand, and whenever a rider becomes more tuned into rhythm, a sense of relaxation usually follows. All of this makes 'Three to the left, three to the right' an excellent way to limber up at the beginning of a schooling session.

The basic exercise

■ Ride the horse on a line 5m (16½ft) inside the track. Move your right hand with the little finger marginally in the lead about 30cm (12in) to the right (near right). This is called a leading or opening rein, with the elbow staying close to the body and the hand being the part that travels furthest. Move the hand three times to the right in this way, in the rhythm of the horse's walk.

■ Then move your left hand three times to the left in a similar fashion (centre right).

■ Repeat this exercise all the way down the long side. The horse should stay straight and not be influenced by the rein because the hand remains light and sensitive.

■ When you can move your hands freely to the left and right, you can add a third element called 'three chicken wings'. Keeping your hands together, open your elbows outwards as if they were flapping wings (far right). Do this three times, in the rhythm of the horse's pace.

➤**CHECKPOINT**
Many riders feel inhibited when they first try this exercise. They would prefer to keep their hands close to the security of the withers. On first attempt, their hand often moves back and down. Remember the aim is for the hand to move sideways and be forward thinking. Once you get the feel of it, you will experience tremendous freedom in your arms and hands. You can then go on and do it in trot and canter, always taking care to move your hand in the rhythm of the horse's stride.

Putting it together

Now try this sequence: right hand three times to the right, left hand three times to the left, three flaps of the wings. Keep cycling through this sequence all down the long side of the arena, until you can consistently do it in a light and uncomplicated way.

Easing off your elbows like this is a wonderful way to soften your hand without losing the contact. You can use it in your schooling when you feel the horse would benefit from a slight easing off of the hand; for instance, when you straighten up out of a sideways movement, or when you come into a halt and you wish to reward the horse for halting well by relaxing the hand but still maintaining a contact so he stays in self-carriage.

■ The natural follow-on from this exercise is to add your other aids to the leading rein in order to ride your horse in shallow serpentines down the long side of the arena (left). From this starting point you can build up into any suppling exercise.

Riding with one hand – a lighter way

As I have already said, there is a tendency in human beings to react with our hands first and our bodies second. However, as riders we need to retrain ourselves to use our whole body as a single tool.

One method is to disable the rider's hands in some way, so they automatically look for other means of communication. I like to do this by asking the rider to ride with the reins in one hand. Riding with one hand takes the strength out of your contact with the horse's mouth, and therefore your only option is to ride with a lighter touch, and to use your body to turn and stop the horse.

This is another of those exercises that is designed to teach you a 'feel'. When you go back to riding with two hands, take the sensitivity you have experienced with you. You will find that less is, indeed, often more, especially when it comes to communicating with the horse's mouth.

The basic exercise

■ Lay one rein on top of the other and hold them in your hand so that the left rein comes out of one side, and the right rein out of the other (below). Let your other arm hang loosely behind your thigh, or put it on your hip.

- Ride down the arena and start making some simple turns. Walk on a straight line, look the way you want to go, put a little more weight in your inside heel, and with the outside leg applied softly behind the girth, move your hand sideways in the direction of the turn. The horse will turn in an uncomplicated way.
- Return your hand to its normal position and ride straight for a few metres, and then turn him the opposite way. As my father used to say to his pupils, 'Turn your body and take the horse with you.'
- Next, ride the horse in a zigzag the whole way down the long side. The horse will become nimble on his feet, and obedient to a light aid, particularly when you do it in trot.

Moving on to transitions

Riding with one hand is also an excellent way to practice transitions by raising your hand. As you will find out throughout your riding career, there is more than one way to ask a horse to stop, and some horses appreciate one method more than another.

■ Keeping your elbow bent and as the lowest part of your arm, raise your hand vertically a few centimetres, as you become more upright with your upper body (left). The bit will come upwards into the corners of the horse's mouth, so that he goes 'into' the bridle, and keeps himself together, rather than going against the hand in the transition.

■ If you want to reinforce the application of the body in the transition, put your free arm behind your back, and when you make the transition, press the forearm into the small of your spine (below). This will give you the feeling of using your back for a more direct transition, as opposed to asking for it with a stronger hand.

■ After a few transitions this way, the horse will also appreciate you closing your legs around him in a soft way, to support him to step under even further in the transition.

■ Change hands periodically, and experiment with having the reins in both the inside and outside hand on both reins.

Quick ways to release tension

In the last few exercises, I have said a lot about contact and the way you use your hands. So what are 'good hands'? Good hands are reliable and sensitive, yet capable of absorbing a fair amount of pressure when necessary. They are the by-product of a well-balanced rider, and supple and relaxed shoulders and elbow joints. The rider's hands influence possibly the most sensitive part of the horse's anatomy – his mouth, and the communication between the rider's hand and the horse's mouth can make or break a partnership. It is almost impossible for a rider to have good hands if they do not have a balanced seat. This is because it is a knee-jerk reaction to grab at the reins when they lose their balance. It is a bit like putting your hand out to break your fall when you trip over. This is both uncomfortable and confusing for the horse. He does not know the difference between you reaching for help or asking him to do something.

It is worth checking up often that your hands are relaxed and sensitive. Here are some simple ways to do this, which can be used either at the beginning of a riding session, or at some point in the middle, when the effort of trying to ride your horse well may have bought some tension into your body.

exercise notes

Use these exercises whenever you feel a bit of unnecessary tension coming into your hands. Sometimes we just need to catch ourselves and take another path so that we do not end up in the same old rut. These playful moves will help you break the cycle of tension that can detract from a good schooling session.

Clenching and relaxing

I find this exercise a useful one to do at the beginning of a lesson.

- On a loose rein in walk, squeeze your fists around the reins as tightly as you can. Keep them like that for about 15 seconds.
- Then allow them to relax, as if your hands were breathing out, though still keeping them closed around the reins. Allow yourself to register the difference.
- Repeat this several times, until you feel your hands wanting to stay in the more relaxed position. You can then get on with your riding session, but take several opportunities throughout your ride to check in with how your hands feel.

Shrugging shoulders

In order to have relaxed hands, you need to have relaxed shoulder joints, flexibility at the elbows and a softness in your wrists.

- ■ To check that your shoulders are as relaxed as they can be, raise them as far as you can towards your ears. Hold your breath at the same time to momentarily increase the tension.
- ■ After about 15 seconds, let out your breath and allow your shoulders to drop.
- ■ Repeat the exercise several times, so you can feel the difference between tight and relaxed shoulders.

Milking the cow

This exercise improves the carriage of your hands and the flexibility in your elbows.

- ■ Carry your hands in front of you in a normal riding position.
- ■ Keeping your elbows as the heaviest part of your arm, let your fists alternately rise and fall, as if you were milking a cow. Let your hands float up and down, leading the movement, so your elbows do not move any more than necessary.

Shaking hands

This is a technique I used to use before I was about to go in the ring, especially if I could feel a bit of nerve-fuelled tension coming into my hands.

- ■ Put the reins into one hand and give the free hand a loose shake. Let your wrist go as limp as you can.
- ■ Then change hands and do the same with the other one. This helps to keep movement and flexibility in your hands, so you can ride as well in the ring as you do outside it.

43

Neckstrap transitions

How many times have you asked the horse for a transition and found yourself bouncing uncomfortably against the saddle? Transitions can become a vicious circle; the more you worry about them, the stiffer you get, then the more you bounce and the more tense, and bouncy, the horse becomes.

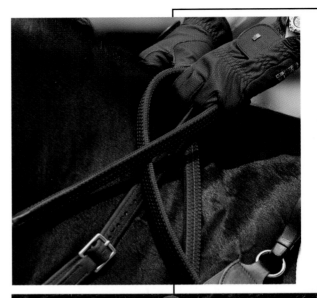

The rider needs to strike a fine balance between being stable with their upper body, and making an internal shift of weight so the horse understands to slow down, while remaining supple enough in their seat to absorb the changes that are happening underneath them.

I have already detailed several exercises that can help you with your transitions ('Legs away', pp.24–27, 'Hold your reins like frying pans', pp.32–35, 'Riding with one hand', pp.38–41), but here are a couple more suggestions to assist you and the horse in having a smooth passage from one pace to another.

you will need

In this exercise you can either use a hunting-style breast-plate, the neckstrap of your martingale or an old stirrup leather. You should be able to get both hands comfortably around the neckstrap, so that it hangs loosely around the horse's neck but without a large gap.

The basic exercise

- Hold your reins normally, and put both hands around the neckstrap (top left).
- When you want to make a downward transition, take in the neckstrap so that it presses into the underside of the horse's neck (centre and bottom left).
- As soon as the horse responds, drop your hands so the neckstrap becomes loose. This is his reward for stopping, and it teaches you to actively reward the horse by relaxing after every obedient transition.
- Once the horse is responding well in the downward transitions, you can add a closing leg so that he starts to step under more with his hindlegs in the transition.
- Holding onto the neckstrap can also help your upward transitions (below). Many riders lose their balance and bump in the back of the saddle or catch the horse in the mouth as he springs forward into the new pace. This will cause him some discomfort, which in turn will make him less willing to go forward next time. Again, holding onto the neckstrap in the upward transitions gives you a little more stability, so that you travel with the horse in the forward movement, and also ensures that your hand stays forward-thinking, so the horse can go into trot or canter without being worried in the mouth.

Benefits of neckstrap downward transitions

- Transitions with the neckstrap help you to remain stable.
- They teach you to apply the hand in a way that restrains the horse's movement without pulling back.
- The pressure on the underside of his neck causes the horse to slow down quite quickly, with very little pressure on the mouth.
- The action of pulling on the neckstrap brings you deeper into the saddle, keeping your seat in better contact with the saddle during the transition.
- Because you are exerting pressure on the horse's neck, he is less likely to brace his jaw against you, and even if he does, you are better anchored, and will not get pulled out of the saddle.
- The horse learns to slow down for the seat without discomfort, and therefore has little reason to lean on the bit, making the transition easier, both for himself and the rider.
- If your horse is rewarded for good actions – that is you drop the neckstrap and release the pressure – it will make him want to do more of them.

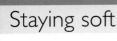

Transitions – looking another way

I have always found it ironic that as a trainer who strongly advocates the benefits of looking where you are going, I also make plenty of use of looking in an opposite direction. However, there is no doubt that sometimes in order to get a point through to the rider, it helps to do something different.

These exercises are designed to help the rider stay balanced and to absorb the movement of the horse during a transition. Simply by becoming better at this you will find that the horse's upward and downward transitions improve because you have become more stable and easier for him to carry.

Smoother halt transitions

When a rider is getting a little tense in a halt transition, I have found it can help enormously to look at something specific, another person or a tree, for instance, that is positioned parallel to the area in which they are going to halt. The sequence goes likes this.

- Decide on a point about 15m (50ft) ahead of you where you are going to make a halt, next to a specific person or object. Look at your chosen marker, and keep looking at it while you apply your downward aids (right).
- Once the horse has halted, you can look straight ahead again. Looking to the side breaks the habit of the rider dropping their head at the vital moment of transition. Therefore they maintain their self-carriage, and so does the horse, and the halt becomes smarter and more direct.

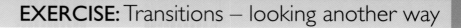

Better strike-offs

One particular upward transition that can cause a problem is the strike-off to canter. Riders will often duck forward in their effort to get the horse to strike off the on the correct lead. However, this actually has the opposite of the desired effect because when the rider throws their weight forward they unbalance the horse, causing him either to run faster in the trot or strike off on the wrong lead. This, however, is easily cured by the rider looking up to the outside as they strike-off to canter.

- Prepare the horse with a light check, look up to the outside and apply the canter aids. Keep looking to the outside until the horse has struck off to canter.
- Turning your head to the outside helps you keep your self-carriage and automatically places your inside hip slightly further forward, which encourages the horse to strike off correctly. Once you have felt this a few times, you can return to striking off with your eyes forward, but still allowing your inside hip to slide forward as it did when you were doing the exercise.

a final note

Learning to ride is a mixture of technique and feel. Untutored children can often sit quite naturally on a pony, well-balanced and able to communicate in an uncomplicated way. Often, though, as they learn more about technique, some of that natural feel is lost, especially if tension about 'getting it right' comes into their bodies. However, nobody can remain a child forever, and technique is vital if you are to move on in your riding and learn how to make full use of the horse and yourself. But, the importance of 'feel' must never be forgotten. In practising these exercises, I hope you learn to develop and preserve your natural ability to feel, as well as learn techniques that will give you the best possible results.

WORKING ON THE FLAT

We school horses for a number of reasons. Firstly, we want them to be obedient and do as we ask. However, this does not mean domination, for the horse that is completely under the rider's thumb and has no spark of his own is a dull ride. You may have heard the saying that the great master is not the one who has the most students, but the one who creates the most masters. Translated into equestrian terms, this means that the rider is the leader in as much as they are the one who decides where the combination will go and what they will do. However, the art of riding lies in cultivating a partnership with the horse, so he willingly takes you there.

Secondly, good schooling will build up the correct muscles and fitness in the horse so that he is better equipped to carry out the rider's requests.

Lastly, so that your schooling continues to be interesting, you need to set challenges for yourself and your horse to see what you are capable of achieving.

TRAIN LIKE AN ATHELETE, OPERATE AS A PARTNERSHIP

Devising a schooling programme

You may come to your schooling session with a pre-conceived idea of what you want to do, based on how the horse went the last time you rode him. Although it is always good to have a plan, I also find it worthwhile to take a few minutes of 'assessment time' at the beginning of my lessons to check on how the horse and rider are right now. After an initial trot round to get their circulation going, I ask them to come back to walk on a long rein. Watching them, I ask myself a few questions that give me clues about the best place to start the lesson:

- How do they both look physically and mentally today?
- Is the horse walking out freely and tracking up?
- Is his head nodding gently, his back swinging and his tail moving slightly from side to side?
- Does he look bright and willing?
- Is the rider sitting in the middle of the saddle?
- Are they carrying themselves, and are their limbs positioned in a relaxed, effective way?
- Do they look as if they are mentally 'with' me?

Use the same questions when you are schooling by yourself, so that you too can get a feeling for the best way to begin your work.

centre yourself

It is useful to use assessment time to 'centre' yourself. Take a moment to bring your full attention to yourself and the horse, and leave behind all other worries and concerns that you might have – these can be dealt with when you have finished riding. You can do this by taking a few quiet, deep breaths in and out or by centring yourself physically, using one of the seat exercises (pp.8–47), particularly if you feel some tightness in one area of your body.

Is your schooling effective?

There are four basic principles that are the foundation of successful schooling. To find out whether your schooling work is satisfying them, ask yourself these questions regularly during training.

- Does your horse respond willingly to your forward and controlling aids?
- Is he in balance and moving in a good rhythm?
- Does he bend and turn easily to the left and right?
- Can he straighten up in his body, and go on a straight line?

All of the exercises in this section ask one or more of these questions of the horse, and help create positive responses to them. They are designed either as a starting point, or as an element that you can incorporate into your schooling.

Rules of the road

There are certain criteria that will help each session be a productive one.

- Start each exercise in its simplest form and build up in degrees. This gives the horse the best chance of understanding what you want and responding to it in a positive way.
- If an exercise goes well, reward the horse with a short break, and then move onto something new to keep his interest up. All of these exercises are interchangeable, so if you have done some good work on improving the horse's balance for instance, you could then move on to some suppling work, and so on.
- It is also worth taking a break if things are not going to plan. Walking on a long rein and letting your adrenaline settle for a few minutes (left) will calm things down and give time for a solution to your problem to come to you.
- Make sure you always finish on a positive note. Remember the saying that in order to preserve a marriage, never go to bed on an argument? It is the same with horses. If for whatever reason, the last part of your session has not gone well, go back to something you and the horse can do well for a few minutes. You then have the benefit of a happy horse. Make sure you take some time before your next session to consult someone more knowledgeable than yourself about what went wrong, or think out what would be a better course of action.
- On the rare occasion that things have got so heated that there is no possibility of doing something well, put the horse away and when you both have had time to settle down, take him out again later to do something straightforward, so that you become friends again.

Change the pace – improve the balance

Take a moment to visualize the most effortless pictures you can from the equestrian world – a steeplechaser midway through a race, cruising as if he has all the time in the world; a dressage horse looking as if he is suspended in mid-air as he extends across a diagonal. These are supreme illustrations of a well-balanced horse.

Improving a horse's balance is one of the fundamental aspects of training. The more consistent a horse is in his balance, the more capable he is of carrying out the rider's requests. As his balance becomes even more refined, he can begin to perform more advanced dressage movements and jump bigger and more technical courses.

Horses are built for speed, which means that they naturally have more of their body weight distributed over their shoulders than their hind end. They are perfectly capable of balancing themselves – witness any horse loose and you will see that they can go from gallop to halt in a heartbeat, and turn on a sixpence. Add the weight of the rider on their backs though, and this complicates matters for them.

A young horse first needs to learn to adjust himself to the added weight of the rider. Then, because much of what we ask of the horse requires power as opposed to speed, it is an inherent part of his education that he learns to transfer more of his body weight to his quarters, so that the rider can use his natural movement to create spring in the stride, rather than length all the time.

Getting a good response to your leg

Before you can work on the horse's balance (pp.54–7), you must make sure he goes forwards in a genuine way. This means that he responds positively both physically and mentally. I see many horses who appear to be travelling forwards quite freely, and yet when they are tested on it, are not mentally in front of the aids. If the rider does not take care of this basic requirement, then any schooling work that follows is of little value.

Make it one of your first jobs at the beginning of any schooling session to test the horse's response to your leg.

- On a loose rein, ask the horse to lengthen in the walk. Look at the quality of his reaction. Does he stride forward willingly? Did he maintain or stretch his neck?
- Provided he has responded in this way, slow him down and give him a pat.

- If he has not, you need to take more direct action. A horse usually lets you know that he is unwilling to go forwards either with an apathetic response, or by lengthening his stride but jerking his head and neck back to the rider when the leg comes on.
- The first response shows the horse is ungenuine to your leg aids. The second is caused by the rider having unwittingly tightened their hand as they put the leg on, causing the horse confusion as to whether he should go forward or slow down.

Whatever the case, it must be clarified to the horse that when you put your leg on, you mean him to go forward.

- On the next occasion that you ask the horse to go forward, click at him in a bright way as you put your leg on.
- Make sure your hands are in front of you and stay forward as the horse responds.
- If his response is still lethargic, give him a friendly nudge with your heels.
- If his response to this is also not satisfactory, then as a last resort give him a tap on the shoulder with your whip, half a second after you use your legs, so that he really responds. Be prepared for him to jump forward this time, and make sure you keep your seat light and your hands in front of you.
- After he has gone forward strongly for a few strides you can bring him back by sitting up and using a light touch on his mouth.
- When you have used this stronger aid once or twice, you can then ask the horse to go forward in the original way, and see the change in his attitude.

> ➤CHECKPOINT
> *Take time to think about the way in which you push the horse. I have seen riders who could make every horse in the world unwilling to go off the leg because of the way they clamp their legs on. Imagine the quality with which you want the horse to respond. For me, that is a light, jolly way, and so I will always do my utmost to make sure my leg aids reflect that.*

your horse's balance

Once you are satisfied that he is in front of your leg, analyse your horse's balance. This is best done in trot. As you are trotting around the school, note what you are feeling. If the horse is fairly well-balanced, that is maintaining himself in an even way, use the first exercise – 'Changing the pace' (right). If the horse is bowling on or running onto your hand, pick the second one – 'Simple half-halts to rebalance' (pp. 56–7).

Changing the pace

In order for a horse's balance to improve, he must accept more weight on his hindquarters. He can only do this when his hip, hock and fetlock joints bend more, so that they can take that weight. You can encourage this bending in the hindlegs by making changes of pace in walk, trot and canter.

■ On the long side of the arena, ride on a line 3m (10ft) inside the track. After the corner, straighten the horse and ask him for a stronger pace for a few strides (above), before collecting him up (left). Moving the horse forward in this way causes him to elevate his stride. It is important that you take advantage of that elevation and collect the horse up before he loses it. At first that might mean collecting him after only a few strides.

■ Making these changes of pace in walk, trot and, particularly, canter (right and below) is like working a spring in and out. It creates elasticity in the hindlegs, which means they will be able to bear more of the horse's weight.

Simple half-halts to rebalance

If you are on a young or unbalanced horse that is rambling on, you need to introduce him to some simple half-halts so that you can slow the rhythm down and get more suspension in his stride. Although the classical half-halt involves a combination of seat, hand and leg in one well-timed movement, this is too much for an uneducated horse to handle. This exercise simplifies the action so you clarify to the horse what you want.

With a horse that is hurrying away, the first step is to get him to slow down his rhythm. The rider can do this in walk in the following way.

■ Completely relax your legs for a stride or two – think of them as if they were made of jelly – and bring your upper body to the vertical (below left).

■ When the horse responds, let your leg come carefully around him again, just enough to encourage the new rhythm (below right).

■ Repeat this until the horse has absorbed the message that he should slow down for this shift in weight. It is important that your upper body does not go behind the vertical because this will have the opposite effect, as your pelvis will go into a driving position.

■ Now, go into trot and add a light touch on his mouth. The order is: relax your legs, become more vertical and take a light feel on his mouth.

■ As soon as the horse responds, relax the hand and softly move him forward in the new rhythm. You will feel, or a person on the floor will see, that the horse starts to bend his hindlegs for this touch on the mouth.

hugging the horse with your legs

There are many different ways to encourage the horse with your legs. To hug a horse with your legs, close them around him and maintain that closed feeling for a few strides before relaxing them, just as you would if you were hugging a person with your arms.

Using this technique in a collection means that while your legs encourage the horse to put his hindlegs further underneath his body, they do not push him forward. If they did, it would be confusing to him, as generally you close your hands (indicating 'slow down') just before you close your legs. However, just as with the 'friendly leg' (p.26), the way you close your legs is as important as doing it. Just as a person may crush you with a bear hug, too much leg pressure will cause the horse to shoot off. It is here that the rider's feel and judgement of the individual situation must come into play.

■ Repeat this exercise several times on both reins until the horse becomes absolutely clear and obedient to this simple aid (above). As a result of this work his rhythm will become more regular, and there will come a point when he will be ready to take a closing leg in the half-halt, to encourage his hindlegs under in the collection. It is important that you recognize this moment, and take advantage of it to hug the horse in a comfortable way with your legs, otherwise the half-halts will lose their smartness..

exercise notes

These exercises are simple but a wonderful way to start any schooling session. When the horse's physical balance improves, he also settles mentally, which means he will be ready for bigger questions. It is similar to practising piano scales. As any musician will tell you that while you would never play scales in public, they are the backbone of a good performance.

Diagonal aids – inside leg to outside hand

Horses tend to favour one side of their body over the other, and so one of the basic requirements of schooling is that the rider works on the horse's suppleness, in order for him to be able to work evenly in both directions. When the horse does this, he will take an even contact in both reins, and this will make it possible for him to be truly straight in his body.

Just like the work on improving a horse's balance (pp.52–7), this is a good way to start a schooling session. It will set the horse up for good quality turns and circles, sideways movements and for going truly straight. Because the horse is supple in his body, he will also be physically better prepared to extend and collect more, all of which builds up his physical fitness and ability.

The basic exercise

The basic work of getting your horse supple is done by getting him responsive to your diagonal aids. This is also known as riding from the inside leg into the outside

hand. Before working on the horse's flexibility though, you must make sure he is responding genuinely to your forward and controlling aids (see p.52). When you are satisfied with the quality of that response, you can start the suppling work.

- On a 20-metre (65-ft) circle, use a soft feel on the inside rein. This may mean gently vibrating your fingers on the rein, or taking and giving in a soft way until the horse relaxes in his jaw.
- When the 'give' comes, drop your inside heel and use your inside leg to encourage him to step under further with his inside hindleg. In doing so he will curve around your inside leg and take more contact on the outside rein.
- You can also encourage the horse to bend by leading out with your outside hand so that his shoulder follows your hand, therefore creating a more pronounced curve in his body.

- When he has responded, bring your outside hand back to its normal position so it can act as a stabilizer to the curve.
- Once you have got the horse moving with softness and complete acceptance in this way, ride him forward on a straight line into both reins, before changing direction and doing the same work on the other rein.
- Do this exercise in walk, trot and canter, always making sure that you ride the horse straight forward into both reins after he has given himself to the inside.

taking it further

When you have learnt the diagonal aids, it can be very effective to use them on a figure of eight (sequence below), so that when the horse has come through one way, you take a small half-halt and change the bend onto the opposite circle. This trains the horse and you to be co-ordinated and easily move from one direction to another.

Working on suppleness

a little help

If you are riding a young horse, or one that is very stiff, it is sometimes useful to have some help from the ground. Set up four slanting poles on the four points of the circle (diagram right). These give the horse something to bend around, encouraging the curve in his body and backing up the use of your inside leg. You can then sometimes work on the circle around the slanting poles and sometimes on a circle away from them, so gradually you teach the horse to respond solely to your aids.

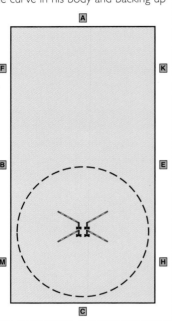

Check yourself

- Make sure you sit level when you are working in the circle.
- Look ahead, so you keep your own self-carriage, and lengthen your inside leg each time before using it.
- Maintain the feeling of space between your lower ribs and the top of your pelvis, as if there was room for someone to put their fist in there.
- If you still find yourself collapsing, go back to one of the seat exercises that level out the body (pp.12–31). Many riders start to collapse in their side in their efforts to get the horse to supple up, but the bottom line is that the horse will not truly give himself to you if you are sitting crooked.

Simple straightening

What is the first thing you are asked to do in a dressage test? Ride straight down the centre line. However, this is sometimes easier said than done. Horses have a natural inclination to go with a slight curve in their bodies, and so straightness is an issue that you will constantly come up against.

It is a mark of successful schooling when a horse goes truly straight and evenly in both reins. Riding straight can be divided into two categories: riding a straight line, and getting the horse level and straight in his body. The following exercises focus on training the horse and rider to prepare and maintain a straight line.

Riding in a school or arena can lull you into a false sense of security. The walls can act like the stabilizers on a child's bicycle, and then when you go out into the open, or are in a dressage test in an arena marked out only by tiny white boards, you find yourself wandering about, and not in command of where the horse is going. Therefore it is important to regularly practise your straightening aids and test that the horse is going on the line of your choosing.

exercise notes

Straightening the horse using this exercise results in a crisper, neater performance. He gets the full benefit of his hocks coming underneath him and will carry himself better because he is no longer falling out through his shoulders.

The basic exercise

The easiest way to teach straight lines is to ride a line 3–5m (10–16½ft) inside the track on the long sides of the arena (diagram below).

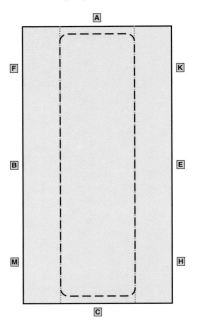

■ Pick a track that lines up with a marker of some sort – perhaps a different coloured plank in the fence or wall, or a tree.

■ When you are on the short side, about 5m (16½ft) before you are due to turn, look towards your chosen marker and then turn the horse.

■ As the horse comes onto the line, apply your outside hand and leg. This means closing them with the appropriate amount of pressure to encourage the horse's body to line up. You can back up this aid by leading in with the inside hand. Think of the movement as aiming to get the horse onto a set of railway tracks, and that you are closing the 'outside door' and opening the 'inside door' in order for him to re-arrange his body accordingly.

■ Once the horse is lined up with the marker, bring your hands back to a normal position (inset) and you close your legs around him to affirm to the horse, 'Yes, this is where I want you to go.'

continued on p64

■ This good start will set you up well for the straight line, but to make sure it continues in the same vein, you need to keep your attention on the marker. Doing this will assist you in picking up any deviations in the horse very quickly. Then it is up to you to apply the necessary correcting aids. For instance, if the horse falls out through the 'right door' (above), you would close your right hand and leg and lead in with the left hand, as if you were opening the 'left door'. Using these aids together will direct the horse back onto the straight line.

■ Practise this exercise on both reins in walk, trot and canter. Ride on different tracks, such as down the centre line, short lines (such as M to B) and long diagonals (F to H).

lead in

Leading in is when the rider guides the horse in the direction he wants her to go by moving his hand sideways, away from her wither. It is a light aid, designed to be a suggestion, rather than a controlling one.

Taking it further

You can test your straightness further by adding half-halts or transitions in different places on the straight line.

For instance, you could trot down the 5-m (16½-ft) track, make a transition to walk when you are parallel to E or B, and five strides later go back into trot. The key to staying straight in all of this lies in focusing on the marker you are travelling towards and being vigilant about picking up and correcting any deviations in the horse.

If you can, find a human being to act as your marker (right). When I act as a marker for any of my pupils, I get them to ride straight towards me and then I point in the direction that they need to move the horse's shoulders. For instance, if the horse's shoulders are falling to the outside, I will point to their inside. Pointing ensures two things, that the rider is looking ahead, and also that there is no confusion about rights and lefts.

When the horse realizes that you are taking the line you ride on seriously, he will start to make more effort to stay straight. Horses also get a lot of security from receiving clear instructions – when they feel someone else is in charge, they relax mentally and become much easier to ride.

Deep corners

What are your corners like? Are they smooth, flowing affairs, or rigid and tense, something you and the horse try to get through as quickly as possible?

This exercise provides a simple way to clarify to yourself and the horse how to ride a soft, deep corner. Once the horse takes his time through the corner, and gives to your inside leg, he becomes much easier to ride in the restricted area of a dressage arena. The exercise is a variation on the diagonal aids exercise (p.58), as it is another way to encourage suppleness in the horse, and can be used at the beginning of a schooling session to prepare the horse for more advanced work. It works especially well as a warm up for the leg yielding exercise (p.82).

The basic exercise

This exercise is divided into two parts. The first part gets the horse to give for your inside leg, while the second part requires you to concentrate on straightening up after the corner. Many arenas have a clear furrow around the edge, which everyone rides in. The aim is to ride around the outside of that furrow.

- Walking on a loose rein, take your legs away (see p.24) for a couple of strides about 4m (12ft) before the corner (right).
- As your legs return, let your inside leg lengthen, and with soft nudges in the rhythm of the horse's walk (centre) ask him to go as far up into the corner as possible (far right).
- Make sure you keep your hands forward. Many riders, even when on a loose rein, draw their hands back at a corner; the horse can feel this and it is where the restrictive feeling in a corner can start.
- After you have walked through several corners like this, you will notice that the horse's rhythm becomes more distinct. Some horses even start to bend in the correct direction, even though the rider has given them no indication to do so with their hands.

coming out of corners

A corner is only as good as the straightening up out of it. As you come out of the corner, bring your outside hand back to normal and apply your outside leg in order to ride straight down the long side or across the diagonal. A good way to remember all this is to think of the way you drive a car. When you get to a corner in the road, you change gear (relax the legs) turn the steering wheel (soften with the inside hand) and then put your foot on the accelerator to drive through and out of it (apply the inside leg and then ride forward out of the corner).

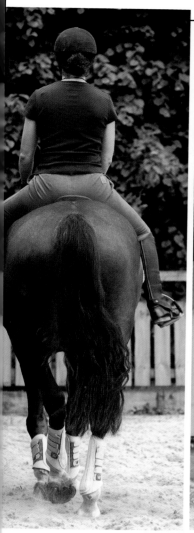
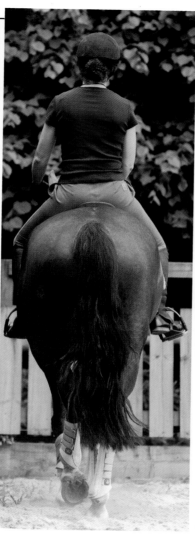

67

Taking it further

When you have done this exercise in both directions, pick up a contact, and do the same thing with the horse in a proper outline. Replace the legs away movement with just letting your legs completely relax for a stride or two in order to let the inside leg lengthen. As you relax your legs in this way, vibrate the fingers of your inside hand so the horse gives in

his jaw, and then apply your inside leg in the same way as before.

Now you must also consider the outside aids. The outside hand goes forward to allow the horse to stretch the outside of his body, and the outside leg is slightly behind the girth in order to encourage the hindquarters to follow the same track as the front end, that is, not to flick away. There is an art to the amount to give with the outside hand. It must be

enough to let the horse stretch but not so much that you lose contact with his mouth. Think of it as water going through a hosepipe – if there is a hole where the material stretches too much, water will come spurting out. It is the same with the horse's outside shoulder. If you lose the contact on the outside, the horse will fall out with his shoulder, or lose power through the corner.

If you are unsure about how much to give with the outside hand, it is a good idea to combine this exercise with the carrying the stick exercise (p.30).

This exercise also works well in trot and canter. Stay alert to the exact moment that the horse needs you to apply your outside aids in the corner, because once you have started the deep corner you must let the horse know when it is time to turn. If you do not, and there is no outside wall to your arena, you may find yourself inadvertently exiting your working space.

Bending around obstacles

One of the great challenges of riding is that the situation changes all the time. Even in the simplest of dressage tests, the horse and rider are asked to bend, turn, straighten, and change pace, all in rapid succession.

When a rider is schooling at home, it can be easy to get lulled into staying on a circle, working away on softness without ever really challenging themselves. Then, when they go to do something new, faults such as a lack of co-ordination and ability to respond quickly and easily show up. It is a good idea to set yourself and the horse tasks that oblige you to change your aids, and ask certain questions in quick succession. That way, both of you get better co-ordinated, used to change and more flexible.

Riders and horses are often better at bending one way than the other, and tend to get stuck in their

The basic exercise

■ Ride the horse in smooth loops in and out of the obstacles, consciously changing your aids over each time you change bend. This means that if you are bending to the left around one obstacle, you soften the horse with your left hand, and apply the left leg at the girth, with the right hand stretching forward and out a little, and the right leg behind the girth to look after the hindquarters.

■ As you go to loop to the right around the next obstacle, change your aids over accordingly.

favourite position. This exercise encourages the horse to bend the correct way, but also makes the rider change their aids consistently, so that they too become suppler.

The exercise does take a little time to construct, but is well worth the effort because it commits the rider to working with the horse a hundred per cent of the time. As the saying goes, committing ninety nine per cent of yourself to something is agony, but a hundred per cent is a breeze.

the set up

Set yourself up a pattern of obstacles to bend in and out of (diagram right). I like to use a block or a small jump stand with a short sloping pole to encourage the horse to give in his side. If you have nothing like this available, you can still do this exercise simply using your imagination. With a young horse, it is enough to have three obstacles down the long side – one in each corner, and the third at E or B (diagram far right).

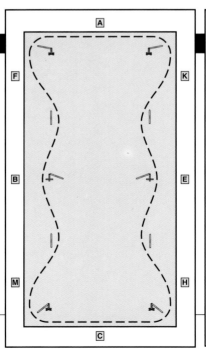

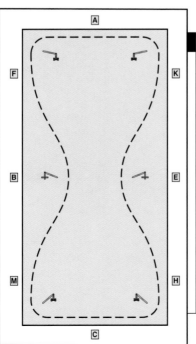

➤ **CHECKPOINT**

Once you have been through the obstacles a few times, go into a bright trot and ride in straight lines around the whole school. This exercise will probably have demanded more flexion of your horse's body than he is used to and so he will need time to recover.

exercise notes

A lot of the success of this exercise comes from the rider being sensitive about both the moment when they need to change bend, and when to change between the exercise and the straightening work. Be mindful also of giving the horse several opportunities to recover when you do this exercise. You do not want to push him to the point of getting physically overstretched or mentally sick of it.

Straightening up

Although the emphasis of this exercise is on bending, it is important for the horse's mental and physical balance that you work him in straight lines as well. Test his straightness by riding a line just inside the obstacles. If you feel it would be beneficial, you can add in some changes of pace, to create more elasticity in him. Then, when you progress to going through the bending exercise in trot, you can intersperse it with work on the straightness in canter, in the same way.

Introducing half-halts

The half-halt mentally alerts the horse that the rider wants something, and physically prepares him by transferring more of his weight onto his hocks. You can use half-halts to rebalance the horse, prepare him for a corner or for going sideways, or to influence him before and after the fence.

Mastering a half-halt is a bit like learning to do a good downward gear change in your car. When you get the timing right, the transference between the ratios is smooth and the power increases. Get it wrong, and the car stalls.

Half-halts range from a light check to a full-blown classical half-halt, the most advanced version being the piaffe. Obviously the type of half-halt and the application of the aids varies according to what you are using it for. A show jumper in front of a fence will often make a check by taking their arms around their body (see p.32), like a spring moving back and forth, while becoming more vertical with their upper body and keeping a light seat. A dressage rider may raise their hands and close them, at the same time engaging their back and closing their legs around the horse. However they do it, all riders are looking for a similar result – a gathering of power and increased elevation in the horse and an improved rhythm out of the collection. If this not the result you are getting out of your collection, it may be that you need to clarify the half-halt to yourself and the horse. I have already described a method for using half-halts on the horse that is hurrying away (p.56). Here now, is an exercise to clarify the aids to the rider.

The basic exercise

In order to execute this routine, you need to be familiar with the 'legs away' exercise (p.24), as it will help teach you how to apply your seat in the half-halt. The application of the seat is a sensitive matter: the rider must make a change of weight to indicate to the horse that he needs to slow down, but if he sits down hard, the horse will drop his back and run from him, which is not the desired result at all.

The sequence of aids for a classical half-halt is seat, hand, leg. Using legs away slows this sequence right down so the rider can be sure of getting the elements in the right order.

- At a specific marker, take your legs away as you have previously practised (left).
- Then squeeze your hands around the reins so the horse slows down (below left).
- As soon as he has responded, embrace him with your legs to move him forward in an improved rhythm.
- Make sure you also soften your hands in a controlled way, enough to allow the horse to move forward, while still maintaining a contact.
- The legs away movement will cause you to engage your back, while your seat keeps travelling with the horse.

exercise notes

The half-halt is one of the rider's most useful tools. Once you have practised it separately like this, you can incorporate it into your work, to prepare the horse for whatever you want him to do next. Look for the times he would really appreciate being asked for one. For instance, if you are changing the rein using two half circles, most horses benefit from a half-halt just before you change the bend. And, if you get confused about the half-halt, you can always come back to this build-up routine to sort it out for yourself.

Taking it further

When you have practised this a few times, reduce the legs away to just making your legs completely relaxed, as if they had turned to jelly, for a stride or so, as you squeeze with the hand, before closing the legs around the horse to finish the half-halt. You will find that you can gradually reduce the amount of time between the application of the seat, hand and leg, until they happen almost simultaneously, as in a classical half-halt.

Circle and across the diagonal

Horses love routine, both in and out of the stable. They become settled when they know they can rely on being fed, worked and so on at a similar time each day.

The same principal applies in their training. Give the horse a routine in his work, and he will become easier to train. One such routine that you can use is 'circle and across the diagonal'. The exercise works particularly well when a horse is fresh or green and his attention is all over the place. Once you have established its basic line, you can add more elements to make it more interesting and challenging.

Trouble spots

There are certain places that nearly always turn out to be trouble spots during this exercise.

■ As the horse leaves the quarter marker to go across the diagonal, his outside shoulder will probably hang towards the fence. You can correct this by closing the outside hand and leg, and leading in with the inside hand.

■ The horse's shoulders hang out on the open part of the circle — where there are no walls or fences for him to rely on. Use the aids described above.

■ If a horse falls out on one particular part of the circle, he is likely to cut in at a place diametrically opposite. Deepening the inside heel and applying it to the horse while leading out with the outside hand will move him back onto the correct line. (See 'Simple straightening', p.62, and the bending and turning exercises, p.58, for a more in-depth explanation of these aids.)

The basic exercise

■ Assuming that you are using an arena that measures approximately 40m by 20m (130ft by 65ft), ride a 20-m (65-ft) circle at A (right), followed by going across the diagonal from the quarter marker (far right).

■ You then ride a 20-m (65-ft) circle at C (below right), before going back across the diagonal (below far right) and repeating the exercise (diagram below).

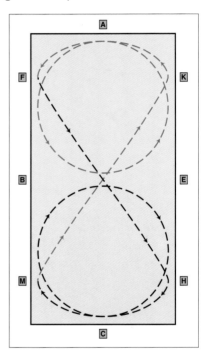

■ It is up to you, the rider, to decide what track the horse goes on, that is to make sure you ride round circles and straight diagonals. This sounds good in theory, but how often do circles look like eggs, and diagonals look like 'S' shapes? The value of being on a pattern such as this is that you can take advantage of the fact that horses are creatures of habit. They tend to fall out and cut in at the same places in the school every time, until instructed to do otherwise. Therefore, as you are continuously riding on the same track, you can anticipate the fault, and apply the necessary corrective aids before the horse starts making it.

Advanced exercises

When both you and the horse are performing the simple line of this exercise satisfactorily, you can add in the following elements, one at a time.

- Ask for a few lengthened strides on the diagonal, and then collect the horse before the quarter marker (right).
- Ride the circle in sitting trot, and the diagonals in rising trot (below).
- Add a second circle in canter at both ends of the school. The strike off and the transition back to trot take place at A and C.
- Take away the circle in trot, so the exercise becomes one circle in canter, transition to trot across the diagonal with a few lengthened strides, collect the horse up before the corner and then strike off to canter at the opposite end.

exercise notes

As you can see, this exercise tests your accuracy and the horse's obedience by focusing both your minds on specific tasks. As a combination, it trains you to become comfortable with making transitions, defining lines, changing pace, just as you are asked to perform in a simple dressage test.

When you have practised this exercise a few times at home, it is a useful tool to have in your repertoire, should your horse come out fresh and unruly at a competition. If he is used to settling and becoming obedient to the exercise at home, all you need to do is create an imaginary arena of 40m by 20m (130ft by 65ft) for yourself, and put the horse on the circle and across the diagonal pattern. He will soon recognize the routine and settle mentally and co-operate physically. This gives you a much better chance of riding a good dressage test.

Remember that once a horse is established in a routine, he also likes variation on top of that routine. If your horse has taken happily to this exercise in a schooling session, stop while it is still going well. Give him a breather for a few minutes and move onto something new. Likewise, although this is a useful routine, it does not mean you should use it every day. That will only make your horse bored and dull. Practise other routines and exercises, and come back to this one when you think it would be useful.

Ten ten five

Does your horse basically go in a nice shape but lack oomph and sparkle? Do you get the comment 'needs more impulsion' on your dressage sheets?

Sometimes, during the rider's efforts to put the horse into a good shape, some of the horse's natural energy is lost. In other cases, a horse may be laid-back by nature and only put in the minimum effort required. This exercise is designed to create more impulsion and activity in the horse.

Impulsion originates in the horse's mind as a consistent willingness to go forward. It is expressed physically by the horse having an elastic, swinging movement, and it is this elasticity that differentiates it from mere speed. This advanced exercise creates that energy by working in short sharp bursts. Short sharp work is always a good tool to have for improving a horse that is a bit sluggish, both in his schooling and his fittening work. It means that the horse is asked to put in some effort, then is given time to recover, asked for more effort and so on. Over time this will make him physically stronger and therefore mentally more willing to go forward.

exercise notes

This exercise is only meant to last for a few minutes at a time. When you feel your horse change, moving forward with more power and coming back with elasticity, go into some other work. The energy you have created will carry over to your other schooling work, and if it does start to fade out, you can always return to the ten, ten, five exercise to renew it.

The basic exercise

- Ask your horse for trot then carry out the following sequence: ten strides of working trot rising, ten strides of medium trot rising, five strides of medium trot sitting, halt (sequence above).
- Be conscientious with your counting, for some of the value of this exercise comes from you committing to the regular, set rhythm. When the horse realizes he is only going to be asked for short amounts of intense effort, he will start to put more energy into his work.
- Keep riding through the routine, around the school, through corners, across diagonals, even on circles. As you change from the medium trot

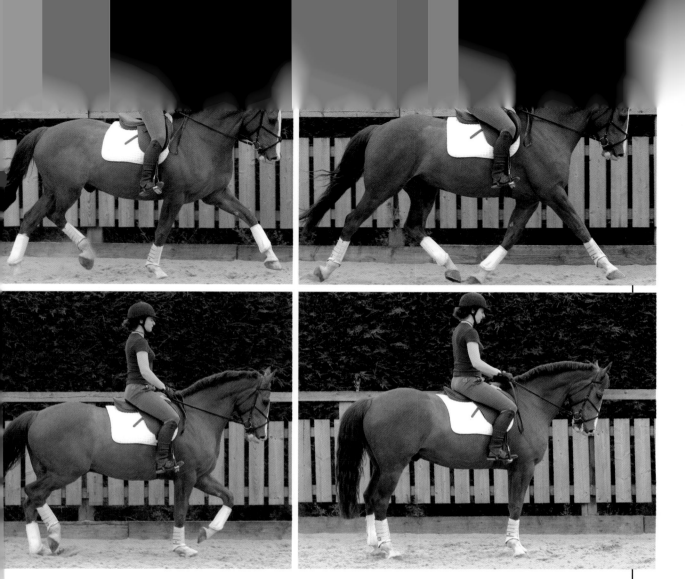

rising to the medium trot sitting, make a point of keeping your hand contact the same rather than tightening the hand to protect yourself from the increased movement.

The exercise works for several different reasons. The horse is asked to push forward with more energy, but halting soon after that has the effect of scooping up the energy, like compressing a spring before it gets overstretched. Repeating this stretching and compressing 'undoes' the horse physically, so that you will find he bends his hocks more and more in the downward transitions, and goes forward with greater energy in the upward ones. Just as when you are exercising in an aerobics class or going for jog and you might start by feeling cramped and lazy, as you are

put through regimes that push you a little further, you begin to feel freer and more energetic.

■ If you are feeling confident, you can also try a version of this in canter: ten working strides, ten medium strides, halt.

working and medium trot

Working trot is the horse's normal pace in trot, and is situated on the scale between collected and medium trot. Medium trot has the same rhythm as working trot, but because the rider asks the horse to lengthen his stride, he will cover more ground. His outline will also lengthen, firstly because his hocks come further underneath, and secondly because his head and neck stretch forward.

Three ways

When he was a trainer, my father often used the phrase 'undoing the horse' in connection with working on the flat. He wanted the horse to be flexible and receptive to the rider's request in his mind and his body.

One way to 'undo' a horse involves combining and developing the standard ways of bending, extending, straightening and collecting. Think of a runner jogging with his knees exaggeratedly high for a certain number of steps — asking more of the body means that it retains more spring when it returns to the usual level of doing something. Muscles need to be stretched and contracted in this way in order to maintain their optimum performance, otherwise they will atrophy.

This exercise is called the 'three ways' because it makes three demands on the horse — bend, extension, collection. It is also quite demanding on the rider. As the rider, you need to be clear about your bending, straightening, extending and collecting aids before you do this exercise, because during it you have to do several things in quick succession.

The basic exercise

- As you ride onto the long side of the school, bend your horse to the outside for a few steps (that is, his head goes to the outside, his neck bends and the rest of him goes straight).
- When he has given in this bend, maintain it and ask him to extend for six to eight strides, before straightening him and collecting him up.
- Making an outside bend gives your horse more room to lift his inside shoulder and step further under with his inside hindleg. Moving him forward underlines this, and then you scoop up the increased power created in the collection.

> **►CHECKPOINT**
> *Think carefully about your aids for this exercise. When you bend the horse to the outside, your inside hand (to the arena) now becomes the one that opens and goes slightly forward to allow him to stretch that side of his body. The hand closest to the wall or fence softens him, and the leg on the same side encourages the bend. The leg on the inside of the arena goes back slightly if necessary to make sure the hindquarters do not swing into the middle of the school.*
>
> *Make sure that your horse truly collects before the corner, so that you are in a position to ride him forward through it. If the rider is still half involved with the collection in the corner, they end up pulling back, with the horse taking support from the hand. Of course, if the horse loses himself, you can always take another half-halt at A or C.*

the exercise in canter

It is necessary to practise this routine in walk and trot to get the mechanics right, and the horse comfortable with the change of bend. However, the exercise really comes into its own when used in canter (below). Through it, the horse can get substantial elevation into his canter stride, which will in turn make his jumping more powerful, and it will also make him more familiar with collecting his canter, which will make him more amenable into the fence.

jumping variation

Once your horse knows how to do this exercise, with some modifications, you can use it to prepare him in canter for jumping. When using it for jumping preparation, bend the horse to the outside and go with him in a two-point position (see p.12) as you push him forward (below). To collect, bring your seat back into the saddle and bring your upper body more to the vertical (bottom). The horse will learn to change the length of his stride in accordance with your change in body position, which can be used to great effect when jumping.

Leg yielding – introducing sideways movement

For the less experienced rider, this type of advanced exercise may have an air of mystery. Certainly, they demand a greater level of co-ordination than simply bending and straightening. In truth though, they are just another stage in your learning and the horse's education, which sooner or later you will need to tackle.

It is a bit like when you are on a fitness programme. If you exercise the same amount every time, you will reach a certain level of fitness, but after a while you will 'plateau', which means you no longer progress, unless you ask more of yourself. Sideways movements ask the horse to stretch and use his body further, so that when he comes back to easier work, he will have increased in looseness and spring.

what is leg yielding?

There are two types of sideways movements: the simple ones that loosen up the horse's body, and the more advanced ones that encourage the horse to collect up. Leg yielding is among the simplest of loosening sideways movements to learn, and is an easy way to introduce the horse and rider to lateral aids. In leg yielding, the horse goes on two tracks, one step forwards, one step sideways, one step forwards and so on (diagram opposite). It is usually carried out on a diagonal. The horse's body is basically straight, his head and neck slightly bent away from the direction he is travelling in.

As with most movements, a good start in leg yielding will ensure a successful outcome. In any sideways movement, the horse must lead with his front end. If his quarters start to lead, his whole mechanism will jam up.

The basic exercise

In order to get a good start, and help you clarify the order of your aids, you can use the following routine. When you first try this, leg yield to a line 5m (16½ft) inside the track, and then ride straight.

- In walk on the right rein, come through the corner with a right bend as normal.
- When you get to the quarter marker, point the horse as if you were going to go straight across the diagonal. Allow him to take only a stride or two like this, to make sure his front end leads the movement, then soften him into a slight left bend, leading out with the right hand, while still keeping a contact.
- With your left leg a shade behind the girth, nudge the horse every other stride. Imagine this leg is connected to the horse's left hindleg, and that every time you apply your left leg you are encouraging him to step sideways.
- The relaxation that comes between nudges allows him to take the forward step.
- The right hand and leg look after the straightness and forward movement.

straightening up

A sideways movement must never be allowed to peter out. Instead it must be finished off in a crisp way. Once you have reached the 5-m (16½-ft) line, bring your hands back to a normal position, relax your left leg, and apply your right leg so the horse goes forward on a straight line. This will ensure both the quality of your sideways movement and improve the quality of the horse's general straightness.

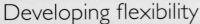

Taking it further

Once you can do leg yielding in walk and trot to the 5-m (16½-ft) line on both reins, you can advance the exercise in the following ways.

- Leg yield to the 5-m (16½-ft) line to a point parallel with E or B. Then point the horse back towards the second quarter marker, and leg yield back to the track (diagram below).
- Leg yield all the way to X, then ride straight forward on the centre line. Change the rein when you get to the end and repeat the exercise on the other rein.

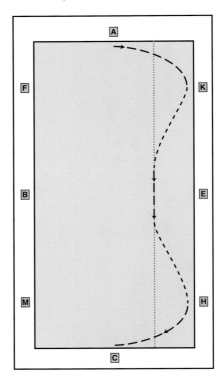

exercise notes

Leg yielding is just one way you can introduce sideways movements. Others include turn on the forehand and asking the horse to cross his hindlegs on a circle. Mastering sideways movements will improve your co-ordination and enable you to have more control over the horse's body. For the horse, it will make him more flexible, particularly in the area behind the saddle, and increase his obedience. When done well, it will feel like the horse is dancing underneath you.

falling out through the shoulder

Should the horse start to fall out with his right shoulder, bring your right hand back towards the withers and apply some pressure with your right leg, until the horse has returned to the slight bend.

Advanced exercise

When leg yielding is an integral part of your repertoire, you can incorporate it into a schooling routine. This is an advanced routine to loosen, extend and collect the horse. Going through this pattern a few times on each rein will engage the horse mentally and undo him physically (diagram below).

- From the quarter marker, leg yield to a line 8m (26ft) inside the track. Then straighten the horse and ask him to lengthen his stride.
- Before reaching the short side, collect him up and go into a 10-m (30-ft) circle in the opposite direction to the bend of the leg yield. For example, if you leg yielded with a right bend, you go into a left circle.
- Straighten the horse up out of the circle, and extend him again, before collecting him up to repeat the routine.

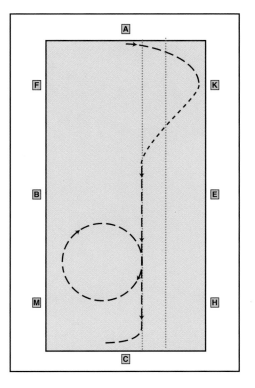

Turn your body and take the horse with you

The modern show jumper or event horse sometimes needs to be able to turn quickly and accurately between fences, especially when they are positioned on a dogleg or are at an extreme angle to each other.

Time is lost and runouts occur when the rider hauls a horse around a turn, as well as creating an uncomfortable feeling over the fence itself. This exercise teaches the horse and rider the pivot turn. It is a more direct way to make a turn, and though it should never replace the way you ride a true corner, it is a useful skill to have in your repertoire because it teaches the horse to turn for a light aid, enabling him to concentrate on the fence rather than be distracted by the rider's hand.

The basic exercise

In a pivot turn, the horse turns around his hindquarters and remains relatively straight in his body, with perhaps a touch of an inside bend, reminiscent of a simple pirouette. Practise pivot turns in walk and trot.

- Lead in with your inside hand and put a little more weight onto your inside seatbone (top right).
- Close your outside hand and bring it towards the withers (centre).
- Apply your outside leg slightly behind the girth to reinforce the neatness of the turn (below right).

►CHECKPOINT
An easy way to remember these aids is to think of the title of the exercise, the phrase 'Turn your body and take the horse with you.' Looking the way you want to go and swivelling the top half of your body in that direction puts you in the ideal position to apply your aids.

- Once the horse has turned by 90 degrees or so, return your hands and legs to a normal position and ride him forward in a straight line for a few metres (below).

- Then make a pivot turn in the opposite direction (below). It is useful to turn the horse one way and then the other so that he becomes agile in both directions.
- If the horse starts to anticipate a turn, gently surprise him by asking for a turn the opposite way (bottom).

➤CHECKPOINT
When you first learn the pivot turn, make sure that you separate it up from bending, so that you get the two different sets of aids clear in your mind before putting them together in an exercise like this one.

Taking it further

The first few strides after a pivot turn are also a wonderful opportunity to make a good downward transition. Because the horse has already stepped further underneath himself with his inside hindleg in order to make the turn, he is in the optimum physical position to go into walk or halt neatly (sequence here).

Start by making transitions between walk and halt. Go through the pivot turn, and as you straighten up, sit tall, raise your hands and ask the horse to halt. When he responds well to these, you can go on and make trot to walk, trot to halt and canter to walk transitions.

exercise notes

These direct turns play a useful part in the horse's training. They make him handy and light on his feet and also help with your more general work on straightening. The horse becomes more alert to your outside aids, which means they will be much more effective when you use them to correct any deviations in the lines you are taking.

You can progress to doing these turns in canter (sequence here) and you can also add transitions. When it comes to canter, turn only in the direction of the leading leg. This means it is best to ride the horse on a square, making a pivot turn in each corner. When you execute these turns well, you will feel the horse elevate after each turn. Imagine this translated into the turn into a fence, with more lift coming into the horse's canter as you straighten up to jump.

Advanced exercise

Collecting the canter

When you are handy at pivot turns and making transitions in connection with them, you can start to refine the exercise in order to collect up your horse's canter.

- In walk, on a 20-m (65-ft) circle, ask the horse for a soft inside bend and then strike-off to canter (right).
- Canter for about seven strides, and then make a pivot turn into the middle of the circle (centre).
- When you are midway through the turn, slow your seat down and ask him to walk (far right).
- Take a moment to relax, and walk straight for a few steps (sequence right).
- Then ask the horse to bend in the opposite direction and change the rein. When he has given in the new bend, strike-off the canter and repeat the exercise.

- Even though you are only cantering for a few strides, find a moment to relax a little, so that you make sure you are not the one holding the horse up in the canter.
- You can help the canter become even more collected by sitting vertically and quietly, so that everything in your body also promotes the idea of 'waiting' in the canter.
- Because he is only cantering for a short amount of time, and keeps changing direction, the horse will lose the desire to rush off, and he will put more effort into keeping himself together.

moments of relaxation

Fitting in moments of relaxation can be applied to all your riding. A moment of relaxation is when you perhaps take a deeper breath and sigh it out, and mimic that feeling in your hands and your legs, so that they soften while still maintaining the contact. These moments are not necessarily something that can be seen from the ground, except for the reaction in the horse — he should seem to settle and carry himself more comfortably.

➤CHECKPOINT
Bear in mind that you should only try this type of collection work once the horse has had sufficient warm-up to loosen up his body. If you start to collect too early in your training session, the horse may well try to respond, but it will be in a stiff and stilted fashion.

The Swedish castle

This exercise was a great favourite at Waterstock. It is fairly advanced as it tests all the major requirements of schooling – soft bends, straight and accurate lines, the horse responding forward and collecting in a genuine way.

It can be done with up to eight riders at a time, four acting as markers (and having a rest), and the other four riding the pattern. Because you need to ride your horse and watch out for the other riders, your steering, awareness and planning ahead are tested, and they are all useful talents to have for warming up in a crowded warm up area! However, the exercise also has tremendous value when used by a rider working by themself because it tests how effectively the rider is communicating with the horse, and if those communications are generating a genuine response.

After this exercise, try finishing off a schooling session with some general flatwork. You will find that the horse possesses a lot more movement for your disposal – he will have that swing in his way of way of going that we all look for.

►CHECKPOINT
Start this exercise in walk, so that you get the logistics clear in your mind. It is up to you to set up the horse for each turn and straight line. Firstly, do a half-halt before the corner, then soften the horse to the inside in the three-quarter circle, finally, catch up the horse with the outside aids, in order to ride him straight onto the long and short lines.

There will be places where the horse attempts to make life easier for himself, by falling out with his shoulder as you come onto the long side, and cutting in on some turns. As the rider, you must quietly insist that he takes the prescribed line, and apply the necessary aids to reinforce this. When the horse feels the rider taking the lines seriously, he will put more effort in too.

The basic exercise

- Start on a line 9m (29ft) in from the outside track.
- When you reach the short side, turn right, and immediately after the corner, turn right again so that you are on a track parallel with the short side (sequence right).
- When you reach the far side of the arena, turn right, and immediately after the corner turn right again so that you are on a line 9m (29ft) inside the track, parallel to the one you started on.
- Continue to the next short side, and turn right again, repeating what you did at the top of the school (diagram below).

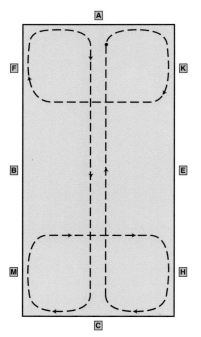

it helps all sorts...

This exercise is of great benefit to a variety of horses. It gives the sharp horse a pattern to stick to and so settles him. Lazy horses work harder because of the constant turning. It is also excellent for introducing fittening work into your schooling – especially good for those times when your horse needs to exert himself but conditions are not suitable for cantering when you are out hacking.

Advanced exercises

Practise this in walk and trot on both reins. When you have got the feel for it in trot, you can make the following additions, one at a time.

■ Sitting trot on the circles and rising trot on the long straight lines.

■ Add in a few lengthened strides on the long straight lines as well, collecting the horse before the corner so he can go through it in a balanced way.

■ Then proceed to canter (as shown): this exercise is most valuable in canter. Obviously the turns become harder work, so the rider has to keep their focus up to make sure the horse stays on the accurate line.

Taking it further

If the horse handles the exercise well in canter, you can add these elements.

- Extend the canter on the long straight lines, and collect before the corner.
- Especially with the jumping horse, the rider can do these extensions with their seat out of the saddle, coming back to an upright seat to collect up the horse in time for the corner (as shown).

The repeated turning puts the horse under some extra pressure for some moments, which will strengthen and make his body more malleable, and the extending and collecting tests his obedience. Make sure that you do all this work an equal amount on each rein, and that you give the horse regular breathers, because this is a taxing exercise, and he will need time to recover.

settling the unruly horse

Like 'Circle and across the diagonal' (p.74), this is one of those exercises that can be pulled out of your toolbox should your horse come out in an unruly fashion at a competition. Because he recognizes the pattern, and because you can make him work quite hard in a short amount of time, he will soon settle and become more manageable, in time for you to perform well in the ring.

a final note

Working the horse in a constructive way on the flat is central to forming a successful partnership and developing the horse so he can reach his full potential. The type of flatwork exercises described here help the rider clarify in themselves what the basic requirements of schooling are and how to ask for them. The work will mould the horse into a positive, athletic and responsive animal, and create a foundation that will set you up for both dressage and show jumping. As long as you do work that promotes good balance and rhythm, tests that the horse responds honestly to your foward and controlling aids, and encourages him to be both supple and straight, you will have a rewarding working partnership.

JUMP TRAINING

Jump training can be divided into two categories: the work that introduces the young horse to jumping and develops his education, and the work of teaching the rider to be a useful and effective partner for the horse. Techniques for training a show-jumping horse would fill an entire book, so for the purposes of this one I have focused primarily on jumping from the point of view of educating the rider. I have assumed that you are sitting on a horse that has had at least some jumping experience.

To jump successfully, you need to stay in a relaxed balance before, over and after the fence so that you allow the horse to focus on the obstacle and adjust himself accordingly. When you are able to do this consistently, you are then in a position to make calculated adjustments to the horse in front of the fence. Many riders try to give this kind of advice to their horse without having the foundation of letting the horse get on with his job; or, in their anxiety, they over-dominate the horse, thereby taking away

BUILDING CONFIDENCE, PROMOTING FEEL

his ability to use his natural judgement. The situation I am working towards here is one where the natural judgement of both the horse and the rider work in tandem to produce the best possible result.

Gaining confidence

Exercises to inspire confidence

The exercises described in this chapter are devised to help you to develop a sense of balance and rhythm in conjunction with jumping, give you practise in riding disciplined lines and help you to develop a feel for the appropriate pace for the kind of fence you are jumping. You will find that through developing these skills, you will gain more confidence and refine your feel for a stride. In turn, the horse will jump better because he can rely on the rider to prepare him for what lies ahead and present him in a good way. Putting all this together helps the achievement of the ultimate goal – jumping clear around a course of fences.

related distances

A combination is a double or treble of fences set with a distance of one or two strides in between them. A related distance comprises two fences with a distance of three, four or five strides between them. The distance is measured from the back of one fence, or the back rail if it is a parallel, to the front of the next one (below).

Rules of the road

- Be diligent about the distances you set between related fences (see box below left). Setting the correct distance can make or break an exercise. You will see that sometimes I have put an approximate distance. This is so you can make adjustments according to whether your horse is short- or long-striding, and whether you are jumping in a confined area (indoors or a small arena) or a large one.

- Have a helper on the floor. Quite apart from the safety issues, getting on and off to adjust fences all the time breaks the rhythm of your work.

- Start every exercise in a simple form and build it up, one stage at a time. This gives you the best chance of building confidence – the number one asset when jumping – and minimizes the chance of errors. It also means if you or the horse make a mistake, you only have to drop down one level and, by repeating something you have already achieved, regain your confidence.

- Take into account the horse's experience, temperament and attitude. For instance, if you have a spooky horse, you might always have to start over a pole on the floor. But if your horse is a bit introverted, always starting over a pole will switch him off even more, and it would be better to go straight into something a bit more challenging. Therefore, use your common sense and make adjustments to these exercises if necessary, according to you and your horse's requirements.

- If you are a fairly novice rider, or could do with more confidence, you will learn most if you are seated on an a well-balanced schoolmaster with an easily containable canter stride. Educating a young horse is a job for an experienced, confident horseman or woman.

Work over poles

I find that work over poles is among the most valuable preparation training you can do for jumping. It lets the rider try out and perfect all the key ingredients they need for jumping without the added challenge of a fence.

If a horse and rider can trot in a good balance and maintain a straight line over a pole, then there is a good chance they will be able to do the same into a fence. In my experience, if you can implant a sense of rhythm in the horse and rider, many of the problems associated with jumping disappear. Therefore, it is always worth doing something that puts you in touch with your natural rhythm, to enhance and smooth out your performance, and give you and your horse a benchmark to return to, should you get into difficulties.

Trotting over poles tests your balance because it demands that you absorb the horse's extra movement, and keep your balance before, over and after the poles, in order to give the horse a fair chance at negotiating them well.

For the horse, working over poles causes him to lift his legs higher, which will build up his muscles

➤ CHECKPOINT
It is part of a horse's natural instinct to avoid things on the floor, and so when you begin this work he may leap over the pole in an exaggerated way the first couple of times, particularly if he is young or spooky. With this kind of horse, it is best to start by walking over the pole, until he accepts it and steps over it in a normal way. Your job is to remain as relaxed as possible and travel with the horse's movement in a balanced way so that nothing in you creates more disturbance.

and increase his flexibility. When he is ridden over a sequence of poles, it will also accentuate his natural rhythm and put more suspension in his stride, which in turn will promote good balance in him.

In addition, the change in rhythm draws your attention to it, and teaches you how to make judgements about the quality of his pace.

setting up the exercise

There are two basic pole layouts for this exercise. The simpler one involves two single poles and three in a row, with a tunnel of poles leading to and from them (diagram right). The more advanced one (diagram far right) has three sets of poles: one single pole, one set of three and one set of five). Lay the poles approximately 1.5m (5ft) apart. Trotting poles are only of value if the distance is set between accurately, and then corrected if the horse kicks a pole out of place. The tunnel of poles will help with straightness.

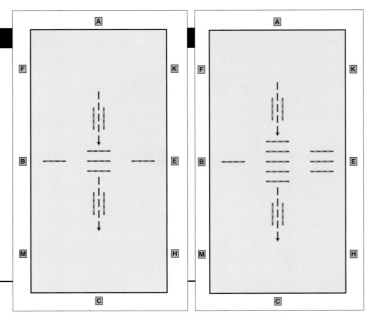

The basic exercise

- After an initial basic warm-up, start by working over the single pole (see checkpoint left).
- Once the horse has accepted the single pole in walk and trot, you can move on to riding over the three poles (right).
- Ride him in the same way you would for any line that you take inside the track. Look at the pole well before the turn, use your outside aids to prevent the horse's outside shoulder hanging out, and maintain his straightness into, over and after the pole.
- As you get near the poles, close your legs around the horse to prepare him for the extra effort he is going to make, and look beyond the poles to help you keep your balance and straightness.
- If you have difficulty maintaining balance, hold onto a piece of mane or a neckstrap, so you stay with the horse's movement.
- If the horse reaches for the poles, or puts in a hop step, regard this as feedback that you need to adjust the pace. Experiment with coming in a touch stronger or slower until you find the optimum rhythm.
- When he has negotiated the poles well, give your horse a change, some canter work perhaps, or make gentle loops in trot around the sets of poles to supple him up.

Taking it further

You can build up this work by:

- Progressing to using the the set up with five poles for a greater test of balance.
- Making a downwards transition after the poles. Trot over the set of poles, and about 10m (30ft) afterwards make a transition to walk or halt. Then walk forward, soften the horse through the turn and pick up trot again. The transitions are often of a high quality because the horse has just flexed his hocks to a greater degree than normal, and he takes that bend in the hindleg with him into the transition.

Learning to live with the horse in front of the fence

Have you ever had a job where you knew perfectly well what to do, yet your boss was constantly over your shoulder, nagging you or warning you about things that could go wrong? Distracting and irritating, wasn't it?

One of the most common faults in jumping is the rider disturbing the horse in the approach, either by anticipating the fence or by giving him unhelpful advice. This interference can range from a small amount of tension coming into their seat as they anticipate the take-off, to hands hanging on and pulling back hard, or grabbing a stride by giving the horse a shove with their seat. The effect is that, just when he should be focusing on the fence and judging his take-off, the horse gets physically and mentally disrupted. He reacts by rushing into the fence or tightening his body, so that it is difficult for him to adjust his stride, or stopping altogether. This causes him to lose confidence in the rider and mars his jumping technique.

All that is the bad news. The good news is that when the rider stops anticipating the fence and, instead, remains in a relaxed balance on the horse, their jumping improves dramatically. In fact I would say that the ability to sit quietly and let the horse use his judgement in front of the fence is one of the major keys to successful jumping. The trouble is that most riders do not realize how much they tighten up in front of the fence, and because of this they blame their horse for a lot of what goes wrong, when really they are at the root of the problem. The following exercises will help release that tension.

The basic exercise

A person's voice gives away a lot about their physical and mental state. A calm, even voice denotes a relaxed manner. A shrill, rapid tone indicates excitability and tension. This exercise uses the voice to change the state of the body. It is especially helpful if you are one of those riders that finds themselves getting left behind or going ahead of the horse in trot jumping.

- When you are about 15m (50ft) away from the fence, start to count the strides out loud. In trot, you count every other stride, in canter, every stride.

- Keep your voice even, in the same tone and in time with your horse's stride, all the way up to the take-off. If your voice speeds up or changes in any way, it is obvious that your body has as well. However, if you make an effort to keep your voice relaxed and calm, your body will stay the same way.

- You will see the effects of counting aloud after just a few attempts. The horse will relax and will become more nimble with his feet, and you will ride more even and confident approaches.

➤ **THE SET UP**

To assist you in getting the most out of this exercise, it is useful to have several small fences laid out around your working area, with friendly approaches and getaways (diagram right).

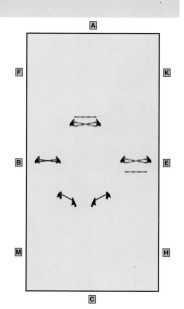

Taking it further

When you have had some successful approaches in trot, try it in canter. Make sure you stick to jumping fences that are well within the capabilities of both you and your horse, so that size does not add pressure. It is important to ride a good line after the fence, followed by a neat circle, so that you are as organized after the fence as you are before it. If you are familiar with the exercise 'Standing and sitting in canter' (p.22), you can add this in, as it will promote good rhythm, another key to successful jumping.

When you have jumped several fences in canter and kept your voice calm and level, finish your session by jumping a small course without counting out loud, and see what effect the exercise has had over your general riding.

variation on the theme – closing your eyes

Another sure way to decrease tension and increase sensitivity into the fence is to approach the fence with your eyes closed (for safety, only under supervision). Once you have lined up the horse for the fence, close your eyes softly and allow yourself to follow his movement. When you have jumped the fence open your eyes again and ride normally.

Keeping your eyes closed in the approach to a fence develops 'feel', that indefinable quality which sets good riders apart from ordinary ones. By not looking, you will sense the adjustments the horse makes in the approach much more clearly. You will also notice much sooner if he is drifting one way or the other, and how much leg he requires into the fence.

It is important not to cheat in this exercise by snatching a glance because it will spoil the effect. In fact peeking often has an adverse result effect – the quick glance causes the rider to do something rash, to tighten and maybe lose their balance. Again, when you are doing this exercise, jump fences that are easy for you. It is, after all, just an exercise.

exercise notes

Learning to stay relaxed in your jumping does not mean that you are never allowed to influence the horse in front of the fence again. It just means that when you do take a check in the approach, you do it in a calculated way, and on top of relaxation, so that the horse is able to keep his attention on the fence and respond to your suggestions at the same time. This combination of skills will create the best possible approaches of all.

Riding straight – a good start

One thing I constantly observe in my teaching is that when the basic foundations of schooling and training are taken care of, many common problems simply never occur. This is most apparent in jumping training.

One of the horse's most basic instincts is to avoid anything on the floor, and he will often do this is by running to the side of it. To get the horse to use his instinct in another way – that is lift his legs and jump what is on the ground – the rider must make it apparent from the outset that she wants the horse to go over the obstacle. To do this, she must ride clear-cut lines and correct the horse should he waver into, over and after the fence. Therefore, it is worth spending some time getting yourself and the horse into the habit of riding a straight line to the middle of the fence, and maintaining that line afterwards. This will build up confidence in the partnership, and encourage the horse to draw towards fences. You can always tell an experienced horse that has been educated this way, for he will seem to 'lock on' to the fences as soon as he comes into the ring.

setting up the exercise

In this example, I am using a simple grid, but this exercise can be done equally well with a number of single fences. On the centre line, set up a grid consisting of two pairs of uprights, approximately 6m (20ft) apart. Eventually one will have cross poles and one will be an upright or parallel (diagram below), however, to start with just have a single pole on the floor between the first pair of uprights.

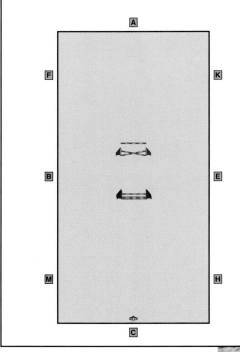

flatwork preparation

As always, check that the horse is responding genuinely to your forward and controlling aids. When he has done that in walk and trot, make some soft turns and circles to loosen up his body. This is a simple exercise, so the horse does not need an extensive warm-up, just enough to make sure the basics are in order.

Another good way to start is to practise the exercise 'Three to the left, three to the right' (p.36). You are going to be making light communications with the horse to stay straight, and so it is a good idea if you are comfortable with using a leading rein.

➤**CHECKPOINT**
Horses often waiver after a fence if they are not actively encouraged to stay straight. This makes it difficult to prepare for the next fence, so if you can eradicate this at an early stage, you will make life much easier for yourself later on.

The basic exercise

■ Have your helper stand on the centre line at one end of the school. You are going to use them as your marker, a point to ride towards to check on your straightness.

■ Look at your helper and then turn down the centre line towards the pole and your helper beyond.

■ Ask them to inform you – either verbally or by pointing – which way the horse is falling out with his shoulder, and make the necessary corrections. For instance, if his shoulders are going to the right, you need to apply right hand and right leg and lead in with the left hand (far left). This needs to be done with a light touch (above), so that although you are correcting the horse, he maintains his attention on the pole (below).

■ Make sure you stay balanced over the pole by being as calm and quiet as possible and keeping more of your attention on the line you are riding. This way the pole ceases to be an issue.

Adding a fence

When you can come off both reins and maintain a straight line, it is time to do the same exercise over a small jump. Replace the trot pole with a small cross pole jump, using a placing pole 2.7m (9ft) in front of it (diagram, p.108). Again, look at the fence well before you turn onto the centre line. Once you are lined up with the fence, look at your helper, and make any light corrections that you may need to ensure the horse's straightness. The photographs here show the rider having to correct the horse gently to the left (1) then to the right (3) then left again (4) before he takes off over the middle of the fence (5). Before you jump, test your horse's response to the leg. Give the horse a nudge with your heels well before the approach, to make sure he is in front of your aids. You will see even the best riders on the most experienced horses do this when they come into the ring, so it is a good idea to train it in to yourself as well. Also, notice how much push your horse needs into the fence. When I was a child, my father taught me to push the last three strides into the fence in this way – little, more, most. This was to ensure that the support built up into a crescendo. How strong the push is depends on the horse and the type of fence you are jumping, but using your legs in this way will ensure that your approaches are positive.

After the fence, keep looking at your helper, and softly close your legs around the horse to encourage him forward on the straight line.

> ### exercise notes
>
> Starting off with this emphasis on straightness will give you and the horse a clear and confident start to your jumping work. Practising straightness in a focused way will make it an integral part of your riding, so that it becomes a given fact that you will ride straight. When you can trust yourself to do that, it becomes much easier to handle more complex challenges.

Taking it further

When you can do the exercise in a satisfactory way over a single fence, you can then repeat it over some more challenging obstacles. You can:

- Jump both elements of the grid, first with the cross pole to the upright, and then to a parallel.
- Take away the cross pole and practise keeping the horse straight in some canter approaches over a single fence.

Work after the fence

Do you find that you can jump a single fence quite well, but get in a muddle when it comes to jumping a course? Often the rider is so relieved to have got to the other side of a fence that they forget themself and become unbalanced and disorganized.

The few strides after a fence are of great importance. When you and the horse work together on these, your competition jumping will become easier, and you will have a far greater chance of jumping clear rounds.

In a competition, the getaway from one fence is just part of the approach to the next one, especially in modern show jumping, where much of the course can contain related distances (see p.100) and combinations. Obviously the horse is going to find it difficult to keep his balance after the fence if the rider is himself out of balance, so if you are having trouble after your fences, the first port of call is to look at what you might be doing to cause this problem.

The basic exercise

One way you can improve your balance after the fence is to look at a person on the ground.

- Position a small fence about 5m (16½ft) inside the track at E or B.
- If you are approaching the fence on the left rein, ask your helper to stand on the right hand side, 6 or 7m (20–23ft) after the fence; vice versa for approach on the right rein.
- Approach the fence in trot and, as you are jumping it, look at your helper on the ground.
- Keep looking at them as you go past them until just before it becomes uncomfortable to keep your head in that position. Then look forward and continue to ride normally. This will bring you back to a more vertical and balanced position, with your seatbones just out of the saddle or lightly brushing it.

Circling after the fence

In the jumping exercises that follow this one, I give the rider something specific to do and a particular line to ride on landing. This is so it becomes habitual for the horse and rider to communicate and rebalance after the fence.

The simplest way to rebalance after the fence is to ride a straight line and follow it with a neat 20-m (65-ft) circle at the bottom of the school before making a tidy transition. In order to do this, you need to pay attention to the two or three strides that occur directly after landing. Most riders, when they think of 'control after the fence', have a tendency to try and take the horse back with the hand immediately on landing. Instead, when the horse lands, sit still in the first recovery stride and then softly ride him forward to engage him from behind. Let your seat be light, so the horse can gather himself without pressure on his back. When you feel the horse is in front of your aids, collect him up and ride the neat circle, doing whatever work is appropriate.

Once you have done this successfully a few times, less leg will be necessary because the horse will be expecting to move forward. You may find now that you can be more neutral, but the horse will still draw forward and be in front of your aids.

Circle and across the diagonal

Modern show-jumping and cross-country courses demand greater accuracy than ever before. Even at pre-novice level, you can be asked to jump an angled or narrow fence. In show jumping, to be successful, you have to make tight turns and ride extreme angles in a jump-off.

This exercise, which combines jumping with circling, prepares you and the horse for those sorts of questions, not only by teaching you about jumping at an angle, but also because you need to be specific about the lines you ride. Added to that, it gives you the opportunity to practise communicating effectively with the horse in between fences.

setting up the exercise

Position the fence at X with markers about 9-m (29-ft) away either side of it on the centre line (diagram below).

The markers indicate the centre of each of the circles, and are best made out of two small uprights or blocks set next to each other with a pole sloping off each of them. It is also useful to have another block about halfway between each marker and the fence, to help the rider maintain a round circle.

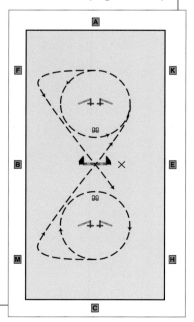

flatwork preparation

This exercise starts with some straightforward and undemanding work, which will warm the horse up well for jumping. Therefore, you only need to have a basic loosening-up period before starting it; during this, make sure the horse responds to the forward and controlling aids, and make some gentle curves and circles to limber the horse's body up for the smaller circles that are to come.

The basic exercise

To start with have a pole on the ground in between the jump stands, so you can be clear about the line you want, before you jump.

- Begin the circle about 5m (16½ft) inside the track at A.
- Ride one complete circle in trot (sequence right), and as you come to your start off point, take the line out several metres as shown in the diagram, so that you can straighten the horse from far out.
- Make a point of applying your outside aids to truly straighten the horse on the diagonal, and then trot over the pole in the middle of the jump stands (bottom right).
- Ride the whole diagonal, before repeating the circle and the rest of the pattern at the other end of the school.

> ➤ **CHECKPOINT**
> *The way the horse negotiates the pole will give you feedback about his mental and physical state. If he trots over it confidently, it tells you that he is well-balanced and in front of your leg. In other words, he is in a good mental and physical state for jumping.*

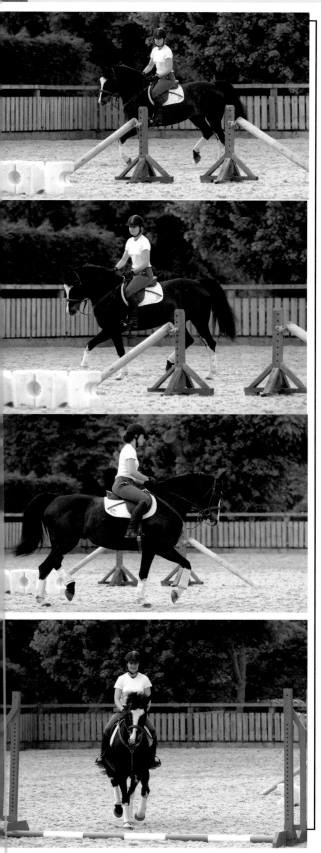

■ Now is also a good time to fit in some canter work, away from the exercise. Test that you can move the horse forward on a straight line with your seat out of the saddle, and then sit on him lightly and collect him up.

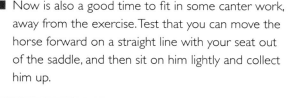

Taking it further – jumping

When you are happy with your line and the way the horse is trotting over the pole, introduce a small upright.

- As before, make a preparatory circle in trot, and then approach the fence on the diagonal.
- Jump the fence and on landing, softly move forward from it.
- Follow this by making one circle in canter, followed by one in trot, during which you rebalance your horse to prepare him for the next approach.
- If the trot jumping has been satisfactory, progress to doing the exercise in canter

> **►CHECKPOINT**
> *Take a break once you have jumped the fence two or three times. This is quite hard work for the horse, so he needs time to recover, and you need time to assess how you and he are handling the exercise.*

over a slightly larger upright.
- Take care to ride the line of the approach the same as you did in the trot jumping.
- On landing, move the horse softly forward to engage him from behind unless he is on the wrong lead, in which case, come back to trot and change to the correct one as soon as you can.
- Ride one or two neat circles in a healthy canter, taking care to ensure that the circle is round and the horse softens to the inside, then put some sparkle into the canter and take your line out again to turn onto the diagonal and jump the fence once more.
- Again, make a point of using your outside aids as you turn onto the diagonal. If you make a defined turn and truly straighten up the horse, you will give yourself the chance to find a good stride.

jumping a parallel

The exercise can be repeated with a bigger upright and a parallel (sequence left). Make the parallel fairly narrow to start off with, as the horse will already be dealing with the added width that comes from jumping on an angle.

putting in the sparkle

Putting in the sparkle is an important part of the approach to a fence. As you approach, you must put the horse into a jumping frame of mind, so he thinks forward to the fence. Do this by giving him a friendly kick or make a clicking noise so you add a bit more life to his canter. (See also 'A John Whitaker kick', p.144.)

exercise notes

Much of the value in this exercise comes from the rider making a clear distinction between the curve of the circle and straightening on the diagonal line, so that it is obvious to the horse when you mean him to jump and when you mean him to circle. The exercise heightens the concentration of both horse and rider. It works by committing them to a line, and this also focuses on the horse's obedience, both mental and physical. In addition, jumping on an angle is a good way to get the horse to try harder over the fence.

119

Introduction to related distances

Nowadays, it can be taken for granted that there will one or more related distances in a show-jumping course, even at novice level. This means that horses and riders need to get used to riding them from an early stage.

Related distances are an excellent way for the rider to develop an eye for a stride. They encourage bold riding, which increases confidence in both the horse and rider, and often results in the horse trying harder over the fence.

This is an exercise that the rider generally needs more practice at than the horse, and unless the horse is green or very spooky, he may become over-confident and start to gain ground if you repeat it too many times. Only jump the same line once or twice before changing the look of the fence to keep his freshness and interest. If he starts to become too bold, take the pace down a little and jump the second elements on a circle, to get some neatness back into the performance.

setting up the exercise

In this exercise, you are going to jump two three-stride distances on the diagonals. It is important to build the fences in a straight line and, particularly in a small school, make sure that you position them so there is a kind turn off the wall and back to the track, to give you and the horse the opportunity to use as much of the school as possible. It is also vital that you set the correct distance between the fences. If the distance is too long or too short, the exercise loses much of its worth. You will be trotting into the first element, at least in the basic stage of the exercise, so the competition distance of 14.4m (48ft) for a three-stride distance is reduced to approximately 12.3m (41ft), depending on the length of the horse's stride.

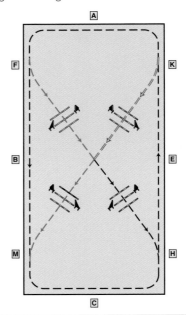

flatwork preparation

As with the previous exercise, this is an exercise that warms up the horse well as you are going along, so it is only necessary to give him a few minutes trotting to loosen up his body, and to use the fences as obstacles to trot in and out of in soft loops. It is also always useful to make some up and down transitions to test the horse's receptivity to the aids.

The basic exercise

Assuming the horse is familiar with trotting poles, it is useful to start with a line of three trotting poles in between each pair of jump stands (see diagram left). Alternatively, it is enough to start with a single pole on the floor at each element.

- ■ Trot through each diagonal a couple of times.
- ■ Make good use of the corner, before making a conscious effort to straighten up the horse as you come onto the diagonal.

➤CHECKPOINTS

- ■ *The majority of horses will hang towards the edge of the arena. Make sure you straighten, otherwise the horse will miss his step over the pole.*

- ■ *If he tries to cut in after the second set of poles, in anticipation of the turn, insist on riding a line all the way up to the side of the school, and make good use of the second corner.*

- ■ *This attention to detail will pay off later when you are jumping, because after a few repetitions, the horse will become accustomed to you asking him to make the best possible use of the school. This is especially important if your school is small, or you do a lot of indoor jumping where the fences come up quickly after each other, because a few extra metres will give you more time to be organized for the next fence.*

- ■ *Trotting over two sets of poles also accentuates the horse's rhythm, which, as I have pointed out before, unites the horse and rider in a positive way and will give your session a good start.*

Learning to see a stride

Taking it further – jumping

When you are satisfied with your line and the way the horse is negotiating the poles, set up the fences for jumping. Put up a cross pole in the first pair of jump stands with a placing pole approximately 2.7m (9ft) in front of it.

- Test that the horse is alert for your leg, then trot down to the first cross pole.
- After the fence, encourage your horse forward into canter, ride straight and change the rein when you reach the end of the school.

- If the horse is not on the correct lead, trot before the turn and strike off to canter again as soon as you can. Make a neat 20-m (65-ft) circle in canter, taking care to balance up the horse as necessary.

➤CHECKPOINT

It is of immense importance that the rider maintains a balanced seat in any related distance. In a normal situation, this means that you keep your seat light and still, with your shoulders slightly in front of the hips. However, if you feel the horse making up ground in the distance, you can become more vertical with your upper body so that you influence him to maintain his stride rather than lengthening it.

Adding the second element

Once you have successfully jumped the cross pole on both reins, put up the second element – a small vertical (diagram below).

- ■ Approach the exercise in an active but unhurried trot.
- ■ When you land from the first element, softly close your legs to maintain the canter down to the second element.

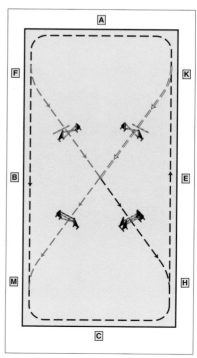

123

Changing the second element

Once your horse is cantering happily down to the second element, alter it, either making it bigger or turning it into a parallel. Providing you are both doing the exercise well, it is advisable to change the structure of the fence often so that you keep up the horse's interest.

development on another day

When you have become familiar with this exercise approaching the first element in trot, you can repeat it on another day, but this time approaching in canter, with the appropriate competition distances of 14.4m (48ft). Bear in mind that you may need to have the distance slightly shorter if you are in a small arena.

Jumping on a circle

When I was in my early twenties, I went to work for a French show-jumping dealer. His party trick was to come round the corner to a fence and, when he was about 12 strides out, turn away to talk to someone standing on the ground all the way into the fence.

Irritatingly, he would still always find a good take-off point. Some riders have a naturally good eye for a stride into the fence, but most need to put some time into developing this ability. Seeing a good stride is a combination of being in a well-balanced and rhythmic canter and picking a good line. Although at the lower levels, the normal horse can usually accommodate being a little off or a little close when taking off, it is a real confidence booster when the rider starts to see a stride, and better still, see it earlier and earlier into the fence. Jumping on a circle is an advanced exercise that is an excellent way to train your eye for this. It also gets you used to short approaches, and for the horse, helps undo his body in connection with jumping, as well as assisting him in containing his canter stride.

flatwork preparation

The best way to prepare the horse for this work is to supple him up using the diagonal aids described in the flatwork section (pp.48–97). Building up his obedience by getting him responsive to the inside leg, so that he takes a good contact on the out-side hand and is light on the inside one, will help the rider shape the circle accurately, it also warms the horse's muscles up in a way that will facilitate his jumping.

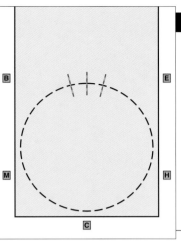

setting up the exercise

Place the fence along the centre line on the open part of a 20-m (65-ft) circle (diagram right). Start with either a single pole on the floor, or three trot poles in a fan shape with 1.5–1.8m (5–6ft) between them at the centre (diagram far right).

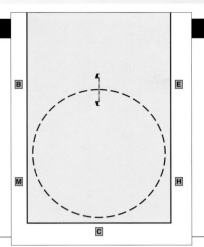

The basic exercise

- On a circle without any poles, get the horse working satisfactorily from your diagonal aids (left).
- Then move to the circle with pole or poles, taking care to ride a round circle with the horse trotting over the centre of the poles. The easiest way to do this is to look between quarter and half the circle ahead all the time (right and below).

- Keep moving your attention, so that you look at the poles early on, and then as you are just in front of them you move your attention to the area after them, and so on. Doing this helps you notice the corrections that you need to make to maintain your line. It also trains you to look at the fence from far out; later on this will help you to see a stride.

127

Moving on to trot jump

When you can maintain a good line and a soft curve in the horse, you are ready to trot jump. Build a cross pole with a placing pole and a landing pole. The middle of the placing and landing poles should be 2.7m (9ft) away from the fence. Angle both poles so their inside ends are slightly closer to the fence than their outside ends. The aim is that the highest point of the horse's arc should be over the fence; if you suspect that he may try to jump the fence and the landing pole in one, push the landing pole out another half-metre for the first couple of jumps, so he gets the right idea.

- Trot into the fence, keeping your eyes on it from about half a circle away. This will help you keep your rhythm and line.
- At the same time, maintain the soft curve in the horse and take care to correct him should his shoulders fall in or out from the circle line.
- As you jump the fence, look beyond it to the line you wish to take.
- After the fence, apply your outside aids to encourage the horse to stay on your chosen track.
- Now work the horse in canter on a bigger circle by going around the fence and, once again, establish the connection from inside leg to outside hand.
- Then return to trot and jump again, either on the same rein, or if the horse jumped it well, in the opposite direction.

correct lead

If you execute this exercise well, the horse will also get the idea to land on the correct lead. If he habitually lands on the wrong lead, make sure you are not ducking to the inside, causing him to lose his outside shoulder. Also be ready to apply the outside hand and leg to keep his body in the correct curve.

Taking it further – canter jumping

The trot work sets the horse and rider up for jumping on the circle in canter. In this you train your eye for a stride by disciplining yourself to take a good line, look where you are going, and maintain a good rhythm into the fence.

Turn the fence into a small upright with ground lines, but no placing poles.

- Establish the horse in a round, contained canter.
- Look at the fence early, just as you did in the trot jumping, and maintain your rhythm into the fence.
- The circle helps contain the horse's canter, and so you will start to feel what stride you are on: if you feel you are not on a perfect stride, increase or decrease the size of the circle accordingly. Do this in the turn as you come off the track, making the corner a little deeper or shallower as necessary; do not do it by letting the horse slide along the fence to shuffle in an extra stride at the last moment.
- Aim to jump the fence once, then make a bigger circle and rebalance him, before coming again.

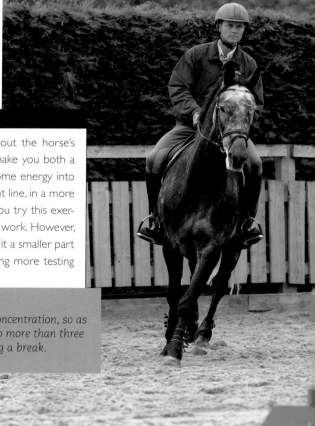

exercise notes

Jumping on a circle develops the rider's accuracy and tests out the horse's suppleness and athleticism. However, if you overdo it, it can make you both a little introverted, so it is always best to finish off by putting some energy into the horse's canter and jumping some different fences on straight line, in a more competition-style of approach. The first couple of times that you try this exercise out, it will probably take most of the session to do all this work. However, when you and the horse become familiar with it, you can make it a smaller part of your training time, perhaps using it as a warm-up to jumping more testing fences and combinations.

➤CHECKPOINT
This work takes concentration, so as a rule, do not jump more than three times before taking a break.

Doglegs and broken lines

Doglegs and broken lines are regular features in show-jumping and cross-country courses. This is where you jump a fence followed by another set at an angle of between 45 and 90 degrees to the first one, often on a related distance.

Like in a normal related distance, it helps to consider the broken line as a complete entity, rather than two separate fences. The approach into the first fence and the line you ride will have a considerable influence over the way the horse jumps the second fence.

This advanced exercise using the pivot turn is another simple way you can educate yourself and the horse about the type of challenges you will meet in competition. Using the pivot turn in between two fences encourages the horse to focus on the second fence as soon as possible, giving him a better chance of jumping it well. It is valuable to practise this kind of line at home, so that when you go in the ring, it is second nature to ride it well. This will make your performance easier and more flowing.

flatwork preparation

In addition to your normal warm-up, it is a good idea to re-acquaint yourself with the jumping turns that are described in the flatwork section (pp.48–96), as this is the way you will be turning to create a smooth passage between the fences. Practise some of these turns in walk and trot on the flat, before you start incorporating them into the exercise.

setting up the exercise

Put one fence on the centre line, about two-thirds of the way up the school, and then place a fence on each diagonal. The distances between the centre-line fence and the other two should be approximately 18m (60ft) following the broken line (diagram below). On a normal striding horse, approaching the first fence in trot, this distance will be enough for five canter strides. Note that you will need to be riding in a school that is at least 25m (82ft) wide to do this exercise. It won't work in a smaller space.

It is useful to place a tunnel of poles on the centre line, just before the point that you need to turn into the second fence. These will help guide you to ride the correct line. Set them fairly wide apart, so there is room for you to adjust the line slightly to make the loop slightly deeper or shallower according to your horse's length of stride.

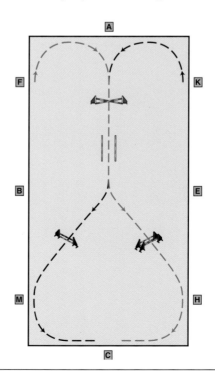

The basic exercise

Start by having a pole on the floor in between each set of jump stands.

- ■ Beginning on the left rein, walk down the centre line over the first pole.
- ■ Look at the pole to your right, but keep riding straight as you go through the tunnel.
- ■ As you near the end of the tunnel, apply your jumping turn aids, until the horse is absolutely square on to the second pole.
- ■ Continue over that pole and around the school, and then turn on to the other diagonal, walk over this pole, look at the fence on the centre line and make the pivot turn just before the tunnel of poles (diagram left).
- ■ Repeat this on the other rein in walk (sequence right), and then on both reins in trot.

Taking it further – one jump

When you are able to ride straight lines into the poles with an uncomplicated turn in between, remove the poles from the fences on the diagonals and put a cross pole up on the centre line.

- Making sure the horse is alert, trot into the cross pole.
- When you land, encourage the horse forward in canter, ride straight for a couple of strides, and then turn either left or right to ride through the jump stands (diagram, p.132).
- Think of guiding the horse through the turn and emphasize with your outside aids that he must go straight through the jump stands.

Taking it further – two jumps

After doing this on both reins, put up a small vertical on each of the diagonals, and repeat the exercise by trotting into the cross pole and taking five canter strides to one of the fences on the diagonal.

You will find that you can give the horse a little more room to the second fence by making the turn a little deeper, or if he is stretching for the distance, making it slightly shallower.

Finishing off

When you have negotiated the two lines well, finish off with a couple of straightforward canter approaches over a bigger upright and then a parallel on the centre line. These act as a reminder of how to jump a single fence.

advanced exercise – development on another day

This exercise can be repeated on another day in canter. Make sure you practise cantering the broken line with no fences, so you familiarize yourself with the line and making a good turn before you start jumping. Also change the distance between the fences to 20.1 m (66-ft) to accommodate the fact you are now approaching the first fence in canter.

The star

This advanced exercise is a preparation for competition jumping. The earlier exercises will have instilled in you and the horse the importance of a good line and a healthy, rhythmic canter. Here you will be able to put what you have learnt into practice in a situation that is closer to those you meet in the ring.

It is worth noting the underlying structure of this exercise because you can use it as a blueprint to create other jumping exercises of your own – you start with some constructive flatwork and then move on to a little athletic trot jumping; you then pop some small fences in canter; finally, you put the horse into a stronger competition pace in order to jump bigger fences and combinations. There are days, and horses, that will be exceptions to this routine. However, as a general rule, if you follow this logical build up, you will give yourself a fair chance to have a successful jumping session.

flatwork preparation

A good way to start a jump session is to remind yourself of how to take a light check. This is useful because it is similar to the way you might communicate with the horse in front of the fence, in order to influence him while still allowing him to keep his concentration on the obstacle. This means trotting on a semi-long rein, and at various points around the school taking a couple of light feels on the rein, so that the horse responds by slowing his rhythm and bending his hocks in a springy way. Once he has responded, softly encourage him forward in the new rhythm.

After you have done this simple exercise, take the horse through a basic warm-up routine, which can include taking these light checks with the horse in shape. Naturally, you will also include work on his suppleness, and straightness, perhaps using one of the exercises on the flat (pp.48–96).

Getting started – specific warm-up exercise

This is a specific exercise to do in addition to your other work on the flat as it is related to what you will do when jumping. It will help create the healthy, springy canter that you want for jumping. It will also remind the horse to be mentally and physically adjustable, and reiterates to you, the rider, the importance of being flexible in your position.

■ Strike off to canter, and be off the horse's back in a light seat for one 20-m (65-ft) circle (top right).
■ Then sit on the horse, and go into a 12-m (40-ft) circle, gradually collecting him up as you ask him to turn through the circle (below right).
■ On completing it, move the horse forward by degrees back onto the bigger circle, with your seat slightly out of the saddle again.
■ When you have repeated this routine a couple of times, you can make the collected circle smaller, if the horse is ready for it.

setting up the exercise

In the simple version of the star, build a fence on the circle near X, with a fence on each of the diagonals the other side of X (diagram right). In the more advanced version (see pp.140–41), these two single fences become one-stride combinations of 7.2m (24ft).

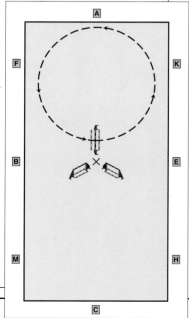

Jumping the fence

By now you should be familiar with riding a good line and looking after the horse's rhythm, and so unless you are on a horse that is new to jumping on a circle, you can start with a fence rather than a pole on the floor.

■ Start by jumping the fence on the circle out of trot.
■ Move away from the fence in canter and then make the smaller circle in the area opposite the fence, with a touch of the collection that you practised in the 'Getting started' exercise.
■ Then come back to trot and either jump the fence again, or change the rein and jump it the opposite way, according to how the horse negotiated it the first time.
■ When you are satisfied with the trot jumping, you can repeat this exercise in canter (below). Remember your lessons from the circle-jumping exercise (pp.126–31). Strike off to a neat canter and make adjustments to the circle line in order to find a good distance.

Taking it further

Now you have done some basic jumping warm-up, extend the exercise in the following order:

■ Pop the small fences on the diagonals, fitting a 12–15-m (40–50-ft) circle in between them at A or C.

■ Put the fences up and jump all three with a 12–15-m (40–50-ft) circle in between each effort (diagram right). When the fences get bigger, it is vital that you give the horse a wake up call with your voice or heels, so that you ensure he is in a positive frame of mind.

■ Take away the circles, and jump one fence straight after another.

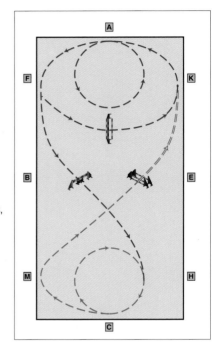

competition pace

Competition pace refers to the action and spirit that an experienced rider will automatically put into a horse when they go into the ring, so that the horse can deal with unfamiliar fences, related distances, and so on. The less-experienced rider needs to practise making this switch from the schooling canter to the stronger pace, so that it is second nature to them when they come to compete. Sometimes I call it 'putting in the sparkle' (p.119) or giving the horse a 'John Whitaker kick' (p.144), but it all comes down to the same thing – putting the robustness and determination into the horse, so that the rider sees healthy strides, and copes easily with bigger parallels and related distances.

Advanced exercise – development on another day

Once you have done this exercise on one or two occasions with single fences, you can repeat it on another day with two one-stride combinations on the diagonals (diagram below). This will require you to think quicker, just like you will need to in the ring.

The house

There is no doubt that training over grids and lines is extremely valuable. However, it is just as important that the horse and rider have an equal amount of regular practice at jumping courses and groups of fences before going in the ring.

This particular set-up is for advanced riders and gives you a variety of options to create different courses, especially if you have limited material available. Try to incorporate as many fillers and bright colours as you can into the fences, so that the horse also becomes comfortable with jumping unfamiliar obstacles.

setting up the exercise

Set the fences up according to the diagram (below). Be sure to position the fences on the diagonals so that you have a clear approach and are not impeded by the wings of the double.

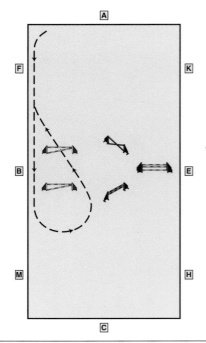

flatwork preparation

By now, you should be able to create a flatwork routine, based on the principles you have already learnt in earlier exercises. Remember to start off with a few minutes assessment of the horse's and your own frame of mind and physical well being, and plan your warm-up from there. It should include testing the horse's response to the forward and collecting aids, his suppleness and the ability to go on a straight line (see pp.48–96).

Getting started – basic jumping

- Start by popping over some small fences in trot. Notice the horse's physical and mental attitude into the fence and afterwards work him accordingly. If he jumps the fence well, ride him onto a circle and check he curves softly to the inside. If he seems as if he would be sluggish into the fences, wake him up with a friendly kick or use your voice to get him in front of your aids.
- Put up the fences to a height well within you and your horse's capabilities and have a few straightforward canter approaches over them individually, including jumping each element of the double at an angle (diagram opposite).

Taking it further – jumping a course

When you are satisfied with your performance, take a breather and devise a course using the five fences. Take a good look around the fences so that you plan the most inviting lines. Good courses have a flow and a pattern to them. Try to imitate this. Although the first course you design may be on the gentle side, for instance taking the long approaches into the fences on the diagonals, do not make the spaces between fences so long that you lose rhythm and focus. The optimum distance for long approaches is achieved by turning into the jump eight to twelve strides away. Make your approaches any longer and it becomes difficult to sustain the quality of the canter and the horse's interest in the fence.

John Whitaker kick

If you ever watched John Whitaker enter the ring, particularly on Milton, he would always follow a similar routine. He would trot or canter in quietly, letting the horse have a little look around. Then he would stop and make a reinback. He would then strike-off to canter and give Milton a friendly reminder with his heels, and the horse would instantly go into a more powerful canter.

Putting on your 'competition hat'

Now you are going to jump a course, it is time to put on your 'competition hat'. Luis Alvarez Cervera used to express this as 'Come through the start flags as if you have already jumped the first fence.' By this he meant you must put the horse in competition pace and rhythm well before your first approach. To do this, strike off to a neat canter and give the horse what my father calls a 'John Whitaker kick'.

This puts some sparkle into the horse so his stride feels bouncy and energetic. Make sure the horse is obedient and well in hand, and that as you jump around the course you maintain this rhythm and energy.

Once you have jumped the course, make a smart transition back to walk, give the horse a long rein and a pat, and assess how the round went. Look at the overall picture, and the detail. If there are only minor corrections to be made, you can put the course up by a couple of holes or change to a new one with more testing approaches and the fences coming up in quicker succession.

If there were some major errors, decide what you might need to do on the flat before you jump again. For instance, if you had trouble getting the horse straight into the fence, you could take a minute or two to ride on an inside track and make a point of applying your outside aids so that your horse takes more notice of them.

exercise notes

Unless you are on a very spooky horse, aim to jump a maximum of three courses. Although you might need more practice, bear in mind that you want to keep the lift in the horse's jump, so it pays to go for quality rather than quantity.

Remember that the time you spend assessing what happened between rounds is as useful as the jumping itself. Take a positive but realistic look at your performance, both overall and in detail. Becoming aware of what you are doing, and what you can do to improve that is a vital part of your learning process.

variations

If after jumping around the courses a couple of times, you feel your horse is getting a little nonchalant, tighten up his technique by coming on a short circle approach to one of the fences on the diagonal or turning back to one of the elements of the double, as shown in the diagram on p.142. This element of surprise often causes the horse to try harder over the fence.

a final note

Jumping confidently around a course of fences on a positive-thinking horse must be one of the best feelings on earth. Remember, though, that even the best horses and riders need to return to basic grammar between competitions. By this I mean checking that the horse is supple and obedient on the flat, and the rider is using their position and aids in a way that will assist the horse. When you take time to check up and strengthen your basic training, you create the possibility for each performance to be an improvement on your last one.

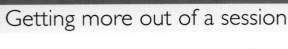

How to approach a training session

My aim with these exercises has been to illustrate the strong basic philosophy that underpins my education and has stood me in such good stead in my riding and teaching. Part of this philosophy includes a belief in the value in coming out each time and doing something specific. If you decide 'Today, I am going to work on such and such,' it gives you a definite starting point, and if it is not appropriate, you will soon know. It is a bit like sitting in the car at a T-junction, wondering if turning left or right will take you to your desired destination. If you decide to go left, you will soon find out if you are getting closer to or further away from where you want to go. But if you sit there dithering, or in equestrian terms, stuck on the endless 20-metre circle, you will never know what to do.

These exercises give you lots of specifics to start and develop. I hope they have fired you with enthusiasm to ride well, and clear up some areas of mystification. How far they will take you depends on how good you are and how much you practise. However, whatever level you are riding at, it will be an on-going process to create and strengthen your partnership with your horse. Make sure you keep enjoying this journey and use any challenges you meet as a spur to greater understanding and accomplishment.

PLANNING A SCHOOLING SESSION

All good schooling sessions or lessons should have three components:

- **The beginning** – where you give the horse and yourself a chance to limber up and then you (or your instructor) assess the situation to see what would be the best plan for the session.

- **The middle** – where you concentrate on building up what you want to achieve, one step at a time. Focusing on one specific exercise or remedying one weakness can have a domino effect through the horse and rider, so that other inconsistencies get smoothed out as well. For instance, I find that if I work on a rider's balance, their hands often become more relaxed and reliable because they feel more secure. Remember also if the exercise works well, to move on to something new.

- **The end** – where you let your horse wind down, and you (or your instructor) sum up the lesson, and you assess what you need to practise for the next lesson and how the horse has gone.

How to get the most out of your schooling session

■ **Be on time** – You will give yourself the best chance to have a good lesson if you are on board, with the right equipment in plenty of time for the start of your lesson. Likewise, if you mean to go and ride at 4pm, for example, do your best to meet that target. Being on time builds trust in yourself.

■ **Put other concerns on one side** – Whatever is going on in your life, put it out of your mind when you are riding. If you are worrying about other things, you will do a half-hearted job, and that will just give you another thing to worry about. Instead, do your best to bring a calm mind and a relaxed, inquisitive attitude to your riding.

■ **Listen** – Giving your full attention to anything is an art in itself, but it is also the best way to make progress. Listen carefully to your instructor, or if you are riding by yourself, assess what the horse is telling you through his reactions to your requests.

■ **Ask questions** – If you are in a lesson and you don't understand something the instructor says, ask. That is what an instructor is there for.

■ **Remember that mistakes are useful feedback that you need to do something different** – Many people are worried about making mistakes, but although when your riding goes well, your confidence increases, it is actually when things are not going to plan that you can make the greatest progress. Use mistakes as a way to identify what works and what does not.

■ **Practise between lessons** – Practice makes permanent. If you want to instil something into yourself or your horse so that it becomes an inherent part of your make-up – that is that you can do it automatically – then you need to practise. Every athlete and musician in the world will tell you that.

■ **Write down what you have learnt** – Contrary to what you might think, human

beings remember relatively little of what is said to them. It will help your progress immensely if you take five minutes after any lesson, or a good schooling session, to write a few notes down about what you did and how you did it. In addition, if you write down particular exercises, you will soon have your own personal training manual.

Above all, whatever happens, remember you ride because it is fun, and because it brings you pleasure. If you can bring a light-hearted and realistic attitude to your riding, and regard any situation as an opportunity to learn something and create a better relationship with your horse, the rewards will be many. I am not saying that everyone can be an Olympic champion, but what I am saying is that if you follow the guidelines above, you can have the satisfaction of a job well done.

Index

acknowledgments

The writing of this book was greatly assisted by many people. In particular my thanks go to:

My father, Lars Sederholm, for being the inspiration behind these exercises, and for exhaustively checking them for accuracy and clarity.

My mother, Diana, for typing up all my father's alterations, and checking my grammar.

My sister Annalisa, for reading early drafts and encouraging me to keep 'kicking on' with it.

My sister Annika, for being one of the models, and lending me lots of Sederholm Selected equipment.

The other models, Fredrik Bergendorff, Clare Echlin and Jonathan Willis, for giving up their time in the middle of a busy competition season to be photographed.

Ruth Wollerton and Sarah Strong, for lending me their wonderful horses to ride.

My friends, Annabelle, Colin, Isa, James and Jim, for their constant support and encouragement.

Olivia Kane for providing us with the beautiful arena at Waterstock, and re-painting the show jumps just in time.

Finally, to my clients, who are always willing to try something new in the name of progress.

IPIKO Black mare, 5 years old, TB x Warmblood, owned by Ruth Wollerton. She has won £100 BSJA, and is preparing to go Pre-Novice Eventing.

RUDETSKY Skewbald gelding, 6 years old, Dutch bred by Voltaire, owned by Ruth Wollerton. Recently imported from Holland, just started affiliated jumping.

MASTER OLIVER Grey gelding, 10 years old, TB x, owned Mrs Sarah Strong. 17 B.E. points in one season, had previously hunted all his life. Preparing for Intermediate Eventing.

BARETTO Grey gelding, 6 years old, Holstein by Baldini, owned by UpTop Ltd, ridden by Fredrik Bergendorff. He has won approximately £1000 BSJA, and qualified for the Newcomers Final at Horse of the Year Show.

CONCHITA Bay mare, 9 years old, Hanoverian x TB by Temple Ash Tiger, owned and ridden by Jonathan Willis. She has completed two 1* three day events, and is aiming for 2** CCI. Jonathan trains event riders up to 2** level. He also produces young horses and events regularly himself.

GAMBLER'S IMAGE Chestnut gelding, 6 years old, Irish TB x by Zaffaran, owned by Nigel Lane, usually ridden by Claire Echlin. He has won and been placed at Pre-Novice level, now preparing for Novice Eventing.

FOXY IMAGE Chestnut gelding, 8 years old, Irishbred by Farney Clover, owned by Nigel Lane, ridden by Claire Echlin. Intermediate eventer with 38 points. Preparing for 2** three day events. Claire has competed from Novice to Advanced level. She works fulltime producing young horses.

MAHOGANY MAESTRO Bay gelding, 9 years old, Irish Sports Horse by Colourfield, owned by Lorraine Whale, and ridden by Annika Sederholm. He has evented at Pre-Novice and Novice level. Annika has competed successfully in show jumping and eventing, and was an instructor at Waterstock House Training Centre.

KUBLA KHAN Bay gelding, 6 years old, Selle Français, owned by John Hale, ridden by Fredrik Bergendorff. He has won approximately £300 BSJA, and is jumping in 1.20m classes. Fredrik was a long time pupil of my father. Initially he was an event rider, winning a team Gold Medal at the European Championships in 1993. He now specializes in show jumping, and trains and produces young show jumpers and riders.